MANIFEST

YOUR

LEGACY

*Your Complete Guide For
Making A Positive Impact
On Your Family & Community
For Generations To Come.*

By

Dean Hanewinckel

TABLE OF CONTENTS

INTRODUCTION

HOW DO YOU WANT TO BE REMEMBERED?

All of us want our lives to have meaning. We want to know that our contributions to the world extend beyond the brief years that we inhabit the earth.

This sense of purpose is so strong it has often been defined as a fundamental human need. A quote from the author, Stephen R. Covey, illustrates this concept. "There are certain things that are fundamental to human fulfillment. The essence of these needs is captured in the phrase 'to live, to love, to learn, to leave a legacy.' The need to live is our physical need for such things as food, clothing shelter, economical well-being, health. The need to love is our social need to relate to other people, to belong, to love and to be loved. The need to learn is our mental need to develop and grow. And the need to leave a legacy is our spiritual need to have a sense of meaning, purpose, personal congruence and contribution."

The earth continues to spin. We appear one day, we live our lives and then we exit. All of us make an impact. Some of us make a big enough impact that the world takes notice and creates a means for future generations to learn of it. Think of Jesus, Abraham Lincoln, Napoleon and Martin Luther King.

The legacy created by these and others has influenced and will continue to influence civilizations – even all of mankind.

But let's go back to the first part of the statement: All of us make an impact. Even if it's not on a global level, will the people we influence or have the capability of influencing remember us? Or will our accomplishments, life lessons, ideals and values exit with us?

This course seeks to help you leave a lasting impact. Many of you have manifested wealth from the circumstances of your life's history. This course will provide the tools to manifest a legacy.

The first section of the course guides you through the process of creating a Legacy Statement - the alter-ego of your Will or Trust. While your estate planning documents will direct the distribution of your tangible estate, the Legacy Statement passes on the intangibles. Your core beliefs, experiences, heritage and values are just some of the valuables that are bequeathed by the Legacy Statement.

The second section of the course addresses the process of giving back to your community. It will help you construct your legacy of helping others.

In both cases, the activities will take you on a journey of self-discovery. To prepare to give of yourself to others, whether it is your family or complete strangers, you always learn more about yourself.

****

In addition to this book, I have provided other resources at www.manifestyourlegacy.com to help you create your legacy. The site is constantly being updated, so visit often to acquire more knowledge and inspiration.

4 Manifest Your Legacy

LESSON ONE:

LEAVING A LEGACY TO YOUR FAMILY

AN INSPIRATIONAL PHENOMENON

Randy Pausch was a popular professor, well-liked by his students and colleagues at Carnegie Mellon University. By the time he lost his battle to pancreatic cancer on July 25, 2008, at the age of 47, he had become a source of inspiration to millions of people.

How was Randy able to create such a profound legacy? It began with a lecture he gave at Carnegie Mellon. The school had a tradition of giving professors the opportunity to present a "last lecture." A talk was based on the premise, "If this was the last lecture you can give, what knowledge, ideas, or lessons would you impart?"

In this case, the premise was more than hypothetical. Late in the summer of 2006, Dr. Pausch was diagnosed with pancreatic cancer. Doctors gave him anywhere from six months to a year to live. At that time, he and his wife, Jai, had three young children ranging in age from four years to three months.

So, on September 18, 2007, Randy Pausch delivered his last lecture entitled, "Really Achieving Your Childhood Dreams" in front of an audience of 400 people at Carnegie Mellon University.

> You can view Dr. Pausch's lecture in its entirety at
> www.cmu.edu/randyslecture/

The lecture was videotaped and made its way to the internet where it became a phenomenon. It has been viewed by millions of people and the book he co-wrote with Jeffrey Zaslow, based on the same principles, has become a New York Times bestseller. Dr. Pausch received thousands of letters and messages, many thanking him for being an inspiration in their lives.

But the public acclaim was a by-product. As Jeffrey Zaslow wrote in Dr. Pausch's Wall Street Journal obituary, "Randy had always said that his talk was in large measure meant to be 'a message in a bottle that would one day wash up on the beach for my children.' The fact that tens of millions of other people ended up watching it was thrilling for him, but he was most excited that his kids would one day see it."

ABC News declared him one of its three "Persons of the Year" for 2007. TIME Magazine named him to its list of the 100 most influential people in the world. On thousands of websites, people wrote essays about what they had learned from him. As a book, "The Last Lecture" became a #1 bestseller internationally, translated into thirty languages.

Randy Pausch created his legacy with a speech written for his children and delivered in a public forum. It was a perfect medium to reveal his life principles as well as his positive outlook on life in the face of what many would consider a hopeless situation.

THE LUCKIEST MAN ON THE FACE OF THE EARTH

Except for statistics in the record books, most of what people today know about Lou Gehrig comes from a speech he gave on July 4, 1939, at Yankee Stadium.

Similar to Randy Pausch's situation, Gehrig faced a future clouded by the spectre of a debilitating and life-ending disease. On a day set aside to honor his career, Gehrig reluctantly stepped to the microphone in front of a full house at Yankee Stadium and created his enduring legacy.

Within the theme of "considering himself the luckiest man on the face of the earth," Lou Gehrig took the occasion to thank his fans, manager, members of the Yankee organization, teammates, opponents, wife and parents. Despite his situation, his speech was not about himself. It was about honoring those who surrounded him on the baseball field. The sheer humility and honesty told volumes about the man and sealed his legacy forever.

> You can read the full text of Lou Gehrig's speech at :
> http://dynamicpagellc.com/Musing/Speeches/LouGe hrigSpeech.pdf
> and view a video at:
> http://www.youtube.com/watch?v=a4msaZTJrTA

Joe DiMaggio, who was present that day, summed up the event: "There was never a day in sports like July 4th at Yankee Stadium, and I doubt there ever will be again."

Randy Pausch and Lou Gehrig each used a single event to create their legacies. They defined the way they would forever be remembered.

HOW CAN THESE TWO EXAMPLES HELP YOU MANIFEST YOUR LEGACY?

By studying these two circumstances, you can find similar elements that were responsible for the enduring legacies these men created.

1. ***Both had a clear purpose for their speeches***. Randy Pausch wanted to give his children a memory of a father they would barely know. He wanted to teach them the values that were important to him. Lou Gehrig wanted to recognize and honor those that he felt had made his life rewarding.

2. ***Both spoke from their hearts***. There was no calculation to create a public image. Many people try to redefine their personal history in order to create a more appealing legacy. Pausch and Gehrig did not. They were honest to their audiences and to themselves.

3. ***Both exhibited extraordinary courage and a positive attitude***. They gave messages of inspiration made even more powerful by the context in which they were delivered.

These factors resonated with their audiences. They were strong enough that people who never actually witnessed the events were impacted.

The materials that follow will provide a process by which you can manifest a legacy that, while it may not affect the world, will impact your loved ones, your friends and colleagues, and even your community.

PLANNING YOUR LEGACY

What does estate planning mean to you? Wills? Trusts? Avoiding taxes? Avoiding probate? I like to think of estate planning as the system one uses to pass his wealth to his heirs.

In the traditional sense, most people think of wealth solely as the tangible assets a person has acquired during his or her lifetime. However, the stark reality is that most people hope to pass on much more than money and property. They wish to pass on their legacy.

Think about it. Your life is much more than the accumulation of assets. Your life is a unique tapestry of experiences. It is your core beliefs, your values, the heritage of your ancestors, friendships, traditions, accomplishments and lessons learned. Yet when most people talk about estate planning, they are interested only in the money and the property.

While attorneys and estate planners have been trained to concentrate on wills, trusts, estate taxes and probate, that is only a small portion of what their clients have to leave to their heirs. Equally as important as the assets are the lessons and experiences that come with the accumulation of those assets. Your heirs can benefit by a better understanding and appreciation of how the family's wealth was created.

Often these lessons provide a foundation of values that encourage a child to help others, as well as to discourage a child from wasting his or her financial inheritance.

It also gives them a sense of being – the knowledge of the wisdom, beliefs, values, memories and experiences that have made their parents and even themselves the persons that they are.

This broader approach may even cause a person to re-evaluate the meaning of "heir," for leaving a legacy can be much more than making gifts to your children. The values and beliefs you wish to express in your estate plan may lead to philanthropic or charitable gifts. Not only does it benefit your fellow man, but including your children in the management of these charitable endeavors teaches them valuable lessons about stewardship and compassion.

GOALS OF LEGACY PLANNING.

Legacy Planning is a complement to the estate planning process and focuses on the intangible assets a person possesses. These intangible assets include family history, values and the stories that define us.

Although it can be intended to accomplish other things, most Legacy Planning achieves one or more of the following goals:

1.   An educational and mentoring process to prepare your children to carry on the family legacy.

2.   A statement of your beliefs and values sometimes told in the format of a personal story, which creates memories of your for future generations or passes down family history, values, and traditions.

3. A manner in which you and your family can leave a lasting impact on your community.

4. A complement to the estate planning process.

Most Legacy Plans usually use the following tools to yield the goals described above.

- Legacy Statement.

- Charitable instruments such as Family Foundations and trusts.

- Family corporations, companies, and alliances with trusted advisors where communication takes place and continuity of the family vision is achieved.

Not everyone seeks to meet all of the goals. You may only wish to use one of the tools in order to meet more than one goal. As you will see later, there are a number of possibilities for your Legacy Planning, mixing and matching goals and tools.

For example, you may create a legacy statement to instruct your children with respect to the family business. The same statement could recount events in the family's history and explain your beliefs and values.

Someone else may elect to create a Family Foundation to provide support to the community as well as teach her children the family's values and methods of managing wealth.

Yet another may combine a message in a legacy statement together with the family corporation to maintain the family business and vision.

In this course, we will explore a number of vehicles you can use to create your legacy. Just as no two human beings are alike, every person has a different idea as to how they wish to be remembered. We will explore each legacy creating tool so that you will be able to select the plan that fits you the best and construct the legacy that reflects your beliefs, dreams and ideals.

LEGACY STATEMENTS

Many of us have, at times in our lives, struggled to achieve success and find meaning to our existence. For some of us, that struggle continued for years while we learned through trial and error lessons that shaped our outlook and made us the persons that we are today.

Was your life experience a journey that led you to this point in time? Or did you one day have an epiphany that changed everything? Regardless of the manner in which you got here, the story of your life holds lessons and values for your loved ones.

As an estate planning attorney, I have had the experience of listening to clients as they strive to create a plan to distribute their worldly possessions after they are gone. Invariably, this conversation turns to their children. How they were when they were young. What kind of persons they have turned out to be.

Many times, these thoughts guide my clients in deciding what each child will receive. Instead of sending a message through the distribution of assets, wouldn't it be fitting if they could put their feelings in a different type of will?

That different type of will has been referred to as an "ethical will" or as we will call it, a Legacy Statement.

The ethical will is an ancient tradition which many trace back to the Biblical story of Jacob, who before his death conferred a personal blessing on each of his twelve children. The practice reached its peak in the Middle Ages and has undergone a resurgence lately.

A Legacy Statement is a publication of a message you wish to give to those you leave behind. It can take the form of many different media. While most Legacy Statements are in writing, an ever-increasing number are being delivered by audio or video recordings.

It is important to realize that a Legacy Statement is not a legal document. It may express your wishes and desires, but it should not be intended as a legally binding instrument.

A Legacy Statement allows you to deliver a personal story based on a theme you select. Randy Pausch used the stories of his life's experiences to impress to his children the importance of making and achieving their dreams, while at the same time, providing an image of a father they will know mainly from his Legacy Statement.

Legacy Statements may be long journals or brief letters. Each is as unique as its author, but most have certain elements in common.

1.   *A Target Audience*. This is the object of your message and lesson. The person or persons to whom you are directing the Legacy Statement. It may be your spouse, your children, your friends, your community or anyone you intend to be impacted by your statement.

2.   *A Message*.   The message is the expression of the purpose for writing the Legacy Statement. You will need to decide the purpose of your Legacy Statement.   Some examples of the reasons people write Legacy Statements are:

- To impart advice to those who follow you.

- To recount a history of you and your family, designed to describe to your loved ones the source and context of where you came from, and where they came from.

- To serve as a love letter to those who mean so much to you.

- To introduce yourself to future generations who will never have the honor of meeting you in person.

- To emphasize what has been important to you and has been a profound influence in your life.

- To explain why an inheritance was distributed in a certain way.

- To tell your personal story; your hopes, your dreams, your disappointments. It may be a narrative of past successes and failures, an accounting of your life. Some writers use the occasion to speculate how they would do things differently if they had the chance to "do it all over again."

3. **_A Lesson_**. Out of the message comes a directive or lesson that you may wish to impart. You can use your life experiences to create a background for your statement of the moral and ethical principles you implore your heirs to follow.

If we look back to the Last Lecture of Randy Pausch, we can see these three elements clearly. The **target audience**, as Randy stated at the end of the presentation, was his children. However, he was able to make the speech appealing to the people in the auditorium and, not intentionally, to the world.

The **message** of the speech revealed a number of purposes. His stated intention was to impart advice to those who followed him (his children). He also gave his children a sense of who he was – by the stories he told and by the manner in which he delivered the talk. He emphasized what was important to him and honored those who had been a profound influence in his life. And finally, the statement was a love letter to his family.

The **lesson** conveyed by Dr. Pausch to his children (and millions of other people) was to emphasize the importance of dreams and how achieving them can make your life fulfilling.

Lou Gehrig's address also incorporated the three elements. His **target audience** was the people who had attended the game at Yankee Stadium that day, as well as his family, teammates and colleagues.

His **message** was to emphasize who had been important to him and had been a profound influence in his life. He honored the game of baseball and the people who had become a part of his life as a result of baseball.

He showed the world that even though he may have had a tough break (his illness), he was thankful for the people and the relationships in his life. His **lesson** was that despite setbacks, you can always find things to be thankful for.

Before we dive into the mechanics of writing a Legacy Statement, let's look at another well known example.

DON'T EVER GIVE UP

Jim Valvano was the coach of the North Carolina State University basketball team that miraculously won the 1983 NCAA championship. He is best known for two things that greatly shaped his legacy:

1.   The famous video of him running up and down the court immediately after the end of the championship game in jubilation, looking for someone to hug.

2.   His emotional speech at the 1993 ESPY Awards in acceptance of the Arthur Ashe Courage and Humanitarian Award.

In the summer of 1992, Valvano was diagnosed with metastatic bone cancer. Against that backdrop, he remained busy, giving motivational speeches and creating the "V Foundation," a charitable organization dedicated to finding a cure for cancer.

For his model of courage and his unrelenting effort to fight cancer, both in his own body and worldwide, Jim Valvano was awarded the Arthur Ashe Courage and Humanitarian Award. Although these events alone would have caused many to remember him, the speech he gave at the ESPY Awards sealed his legacy.

In many ways this speech was the consummate Legacy Statement. In the short time he was behind the podium, he stated his final life's ambition to help cure cancer, announced the creation of the V Foundation, shared a story from his life, and imparted a lesson with his theory of living a full life.

After experiencing this presentation, even someone who had never previously heard of him, knew what Jim Valvano was about.

He attributed his parents for his passion in life and explained:

"To me, there are three things we all should do everyday. We should do this every day of our lives. Number one is laugh. You should laugh everyday. Number two is think. You should spend some time in thought. And number three is, you should have your emotions moved to tears, could be happiness or joy. But think about it. If you laugh, you think and you cry, that's a full day. That's a heck of a day. You do that seven days a week, you're going to have something special."

Valvano then gave a humorous account of the first locker room speech he ever made to a team. He next spoke about courage, stating that the courage in his family came from his wife, his three daughters and his mother; all of whom were present at the ceremony.

He guaranteed his legacy with the next part of the speech:

"Now, I look at where I am now and I know what I want to do. What I would like to be able to do is spend whatever time I have left and to give, and maybe some hope to others . . . We are starting the Jimmy V Foundation for Cancer Research. And its motto is 'Don't give up, don't ever give up.' And that's what I'm going to try to do every minute that I have left. I will thank God for the day and the moments I have."

Valvano then closed out his speech with a blend of courage and inspiration:

"Cancer can take away all my physical ability. It cannot touch my mind. It cannot touch my heart. It cannot touch my soul. And those three things are going to carry on forever."

Coach Valvano's speech can be seen in its entirety at: http://www.youtube.com/watch?v=ePXlkqkFH6s

LESSON TWO:

WRITING YOUR LEGACY STATEMENT

The process you are about to embark upon has the potential to be as valuable to you as the finished product will be to your heirs. In writing a Legacy Statement you will come face to face with your life and your mortality. You will learn a great deal about yourself: what is most important to you, your core values and beliefs, and how you want others to remember you. You will identify the essential truths you have learned in your lifetime, relish your accomplishments and face up to your failures. By doing so, you will gain a fuller understanding of that unique individual that is you.

The benefits to your family and loved ones are considerable. Unlike traditional wills that transfer worldly possessions, a Legacy Statement bequeaths values, ideas, beliefs and experiences. As an estate planning tool, it can explain why certain bequests and distributions were made. As a legacy statement, it can provide your loved ones with a gift that shares the things that matter most to you. It preserves the traditions and stories that define you and your ancestors. And most importantly, it serves as a lasting heritage to help your family and future generations remember you as the person you are.

The steps outlined in this course will provide you with a working procedure and framework to create your Legacy Statement.

Your Legacy Statement doesn't need to be written in an hour, a day, a week, or even a year. Work at your own pace. This is your legacy. The goal of this exercise is to have you reflect on your life, your values and beliefs. This takes time.

STEP ONE:

IDENTIFY THE TARGET FOR YOUR MESSAGE.

Who is your audience? The first step in writing your Legacy Statement is to decide whom you are directing your message to. This may be a spouse, your children, a parent, friend or other person or people important to you. Identifying your audience is more than just naming a person or people. You must match that person with the message you intend to deliver.

An effective exercise is to mentally picture yourself speaking to your target audience. Visualize delivering your message and also the reaction of your audience. Even if your target audience is intended to be generations later, you should do this exercise. It may require a little more imagination. For example, picture great-grandchildren as younger versions of your children or grandchildren. By doing this, you can set the tone for your Legacy Statement.

Now that you have identified the target for your message, you should identify **with** that person or people. What circumstances of their lives do you wish to address?

In Randy Pausch's case, his children were the target for his message. He pictured them at an age where they would want to know more about their father. His lecture was, in effect, a compilation of stories and conversations he would have had with his children to create a bond and pass his wisdom, values and ideals to them.

If you can put yourself in your target audience's place, the empathy that is created will cause your audience to relate to your message and increase its effectiveness.

LEGACY WRITING EXERCISE -- Write down the names or description of your target audience. Picture an image of your audience and describe that image in writing. Were the people or person in your audience listening to you speak? Or were they reading your message? How was he or she or, if more than one person, they dressed? How old were they in your image? What was the setting? What was their reaction to the message? Be as vivid and detailed as possible in your writing. Don't worry about grammar, sentence structure or even if it will make sense to someone else. These notes are for you. You want to preserve your feelings and emotions as completely as possible, so when you sit down to write your Legacy Statement, you can recreate the emotional impact for your audience.

This is going to take some work and putting your feelings into writing may be hard for you to do at first. But I promise, the effort you put into this exercise will be well worth it.

STEP TWO:

IDENTIFY THE PURPOSE.

Why are you writing your Legacy Statement? The idea of planning your legacy resonated with you. Otherwise, you wouldn't have bought this course. Think back on the ideas and emotions you had when first introduced to this topic. Write them down. These are the seeds of your purpose for writing a legacy statement.

A look at the benefits of the Legacy Statement may help you state the purpose. Although most writers are seeking one or more of these benefits, they certainly don't comprise all of the benefits of a Legacy Statement.

1. ***Provide Insight - Why You Did Things.*** Many times, this leads to an unexpected benefit. While you seek to have others understand you, you gain an insight into your own life. Through this process, many people discover underlying emotions or beliefs that explain why they did certain things. These discoveries may fill in a gap in the writer's understanding or may even completely change their understanding.

2. ***Provide a perspective of your life.*** Your actions cannot be fully understood until they are viewed within the atmosphere and circumstances in which they occurred.

3. **Share Values.** You can pass your beliefs, ethics and values to your heirs and loved ones.

4. **Have an impact on your family for generations.** Your actions, beliefs and accomplishments retain their relevance and become a part of your family's history.

5. **Acknowledge people who have shaped your life.** This is a powerful way to thank the people who have mentored you, provided you with opportunity or who have meant so much to you during your life.

Write down the purpose or purposes for creating your Legacy Statement. Write down any that come to you. You can modify or eliminate them later. The important thing is to fully explore all possible purposes you may have for writing your Legacy Statement.

Next, for each purpose you need to ask yourself why that purpose is important to you.

As an example, suppose one of your purposes is to give insight to your son as to why you did a certain thing. The answer to Why? may be as follows:

"Because I see in my son a lot of me when I was at that age. I can personally relate to the manner in which he is handling a certain situation. By explaining the lessons I learned through painful trial and error, I can help him avoid that process and the frustrations that go along with it."

In some cases, you may have already done things to help give your son your experience and insights to a problem. The reason for your purpose would then be to explain why you did those things.

Another example:

Purpose: to acknowledge your parents for their contributions to your life.

Why: First, an expression of love and gratitude that you may not have been able to give when they were alive. Second, it is important to you that your children and future generations know your parents and the selfless way they lived their lives. You wish to extol their legacy.

Many people are tempted to skip this step. They believe that they know the purpose for their Legacy Statement intuitively. I'm going to suggest that you resist this temptation. This exercise is extremely important because the quality of your Legacy Statement will be far superior if you can delve into your reasons for writing it.

By knowing the underlying reasons behind your purpose, you can move from a superficial statement to one that speaks from the heart and fully addresses those issues that are important.

Finally, picture the reaction or emotion you are striving for your target audience to reach. By visualizing their reaction, you can better tailor your writing to reach that result.

Remember, the purpose is why you are writing. Make sure your Legacy Statement fully addresses it.

STEP THREE:

DEVELOP A THEME.

Once you have identified the purpose for your Legacy Statement, the next step is to develop a manner to express that purpose.

This is accomplished with the theme. The theme of your Legacy Statement encompasses the format you will use. Popular formats include letters, stories and directives. You should use the format that will best deliver your message to your target market and best reflect your personality.

The theme is also the context in which you will deliver your message. Some examples of possible themes are:

1. *Advice and Guidance.* Your message can be delivered to your target audience through a letter or

other writing providing your advice and guidance on how to deal with a particular issue. You may wish to use stories of personal experiences to show empathy with your audience and to tell how you approached the same issue. The writing can pass on your experience; the mistakes you made, the importance of persistence, and the actions that led to success.

2. **Values.** One of the most important and valuable gifts you can make to your heirs is the explanation of your morals and values. Advice and guidance can help someone face a particular situation, but your values provide a basis for approaching everything they may encounter in their lives.

3. **Estate Planning.** Your will, trust, insurance and other vehicles are designed to provide a financial legacy. Your Legacy Statement provides an opportunity for you to explain why you prepared your estate plan the way you did. It also allows you to impart your ideas and philosophy for managing wealth.

Warren Buffet has already made much of his estate planning and his philosophy of it known to his family and the public. His statement regarding his children's inheritance has been adopted by many people, *"The perfect amount of money to leave children is enough money so that they would feel they could do anything, but not so much that they could do nothing."*

Your Legacy Statement is a chance to teach your heirs about charitable giving and stewardship. An increasing number of families have created Family Foundations or other charitable giving programs. The origin of these programs along with the goals and values behind them can be expressed in your Legacy Statement. Later in this course, we will address Family Foundations and Charitable Gifting.

4. ***Family History and Tradition.*** In past generations, families tended to remain in the same geographical area and maintain constant contact. Family traditions were passed on personally through word of mouth, experiencing those traditions, and through rituals. More recently, families have spread apart. Offspring move across the country to pursue careers. Family gatherings become less frequent.

A Legacy Statement is an ideal means to preserve the traditions and history of the family that may otherwise be diluted. While some family rituals may fade away, the significance and history of the family traditions can be saved. Stories of the prior generations and personal accounts of the importance of the family's history and tradition can help replace what was once bequeathed by experience.

5. ***Expression of Love.*** The Legacy Statement is the perfect vehicle for telling your children or other family members or friends how much you love them and what they have meant to you. You can express your gratitude to those who have impacted your life.

These statements are treasured by the recipients. It is a deeply personal connection between you and them that endures beyond your lifetime. It is a final chance to mend fences, to right wrongs, to forgive and to clarify your feelings. You should never underestimate the value of a heartfelt message given in your Legacy Statement.

6. ***Personal History.*** This is an opportunity to tell your story to those who follow you. Who were you? What were your accomplishments? Your trials and tribulations? Your joys and sorrows? What was important to you? What people and events influenced you? How do you wish to be remembered?

A Legacy Statement provides a means for you to introduce yourself to future generations and to maintain your relevance to the family or community.

7. ***Requests and Desires for the Future.*** Is there unfinished work that you wish to pass on? Is there a purpose for your tangible estate that you want your heirs to pursue? Your Legacy Statement is an opportunity to express these wishes.

Many use Legacy Statements to pass along family roles. It can be a request as simple as 'take care of your Mother," or it can be detailed instructions of how to administer a charitable gift.

This is the point in the process where many writers get stuck. Many of us instinctively know who we want to write to and the purpose of that writing. But when it comes time to put pen to paper, it becomes extremely difficult.

In order to help you develop your theme, I have included a writing exercise to assist in framing and expanding ideas. This exercise is commonly referred to as "writing prompts." Sometimes it is easier to write when responding to direct questions. You will find that the writing you do in this exercise will provide much of the exact wording that you will use in your Legacy Statement.

In addition to the writing prompts, I have provided a number of inspirational quotes that relate to the subject of leaving a legacy and writing.

The following questions are intended to cause you to reflect on different aspects of your life. Please read all of the questions before you begin to answer any of them. Then go back and answer those that you wish. Feel free to skip any questions. Also, feel free to expound on a question; even if it does not directly relate to the question or takes you off on a tangent. The decisions you make regarding which questions to answer and the manner in which you answer them will begin to develop a theme for your Legacy Statement.

WRITING PROMPTS:

FAMILY HERITAGE

1. Who gave you your name and why?

2. What are your parents' names? What are your favorite memories of each? What makes those memories special?

3. What are some of the most important values that were passed on to you by your parents?

4. What relative (other than your parents), friend, mentor, etc. had the biggest influence on your childhood? How?

5. What are your brothers' and sisters' names? Describe a special memory about each brother and sister.

6. Describe your childhood home and some favorite memories of it.

7. What career or jobs did your parents have? What do you remember most about their working?

8. Describe a memorable family vacation.

9. What role does your family heritage play in your life now? What lessons or experiences regarding your family heritage do you wish to pass on?

10. Did tragedy ever strike your family? If so, how did it affect you?

11. What family customs or traditions would you like to pass on to your children or grandchildren? Why are they important to you?

GROWING UP

1. Who were your childhood heroes? Why?

2. Who was your most influential teacher? How did he or she affect your life, values or beliefs?

3. Who was your best friend growing up? Describe some fond memories of times together.

4. What were some fads from your school days? Did you participate in them? Why or why not?

5. What subjects in school were you attracted to? Why? How did they shape your life?

6. Describe an important lesson you learned in your early life? How has this lesson affected your subsequent life?

ADULTHOOD

1. How did you meet your spouse (or significant other)? What attracted you to him or her?

2. How did you choose your career? Is it a career you would want your children or grandchildren to choose? Why or why not?

3. What is your favorite book/movie? Why? How has it impacted your life?

4. Write a favorite poem, writing or quote that has been especially meaningful in your life. How has it been meaningful?

5. Describe your passions in life.

6. When you became a new parent, what was your greatest fear? Your greatest joy?

7. Describe the most vivid memory of your children's childhoods.

8. Tell about a special outing you took as an adult with your father, mother, child or spouse. What makes this a special memory?

9. Who are your adult heroes? Why?

10.	Other than family, what are the most important relationships in your life?

11.	What are your proudest accomplishments?

12.	What values do consider to be important in business? Describe an experience to illustrate.

13.	How do you define success?

14.	What are your goals for the rest of your life?

SERVING OTHERS

1.	How do you enjoy helping other people? Share a story of a time when you helped someone in need?

2.	What are your beliefs on community service? How do you serve your community?

3.	What are your views on philanthropy?

4.	What are some causes, issues or organizations that you value? How have they affected your life?

5.	How do you want to be remembered in your community?

6.	As of today, how do you think you will be remembered in your community?

7. How would you advise your children or grandchildren to make a difference in their community and the lives of others?

SPIRITUALITY.

1. What are your religious beliefs? How did they come about?

2. What books, readings, verses, etc. have influenced your life? How?

3. How have your religious beliefs changed, strengthened, or evolved during your lifetime?

4. Who was your most memorable pastor or Sunday School teacher? Why?

5. What events in your life have strengthened or weakened your belief in prayer?

6. Did you ever feel that God had a special calling on your life?

7. What spiritual legacy would you like to leave for others? Why is this important to you?

Review the writings you have made during the exercise. Some paragraphs will relate to others, either in the message they portray, the feelings you get from reading them or some other way. Put these paragraphs together. Now, in writing, describe the relationship that these paragraphs have with each other. If this leads to other thoughts that you consider important, write them down also. At this time a theme or a number of themes should begin to emerge. Try to describe those themes in writing.

If you have not recognized a theme at this time, review the writings again. Sometimes it is a good idea to set this project aside for a few days or weeks before the second review. It will take some of the pressure of writing off of you and give you an opportunity to reflect on your motives for writing a Legacy Statement. Another method is to imagine that you are meeting one of your ancestors. What questions will you want to ask him? Those will likely be the things your descendants will want to know about you.

INSPIRATIONAL QUOTES.

Quotations have the ability to inspire like nothing else. Great quotes are much more than the "turning of a phrase." They impart ideas while, at the same time, they invoke emotion. They have the capability of simultaneously educating and motivating. A truly great quote can move people with a few words in ways that an entire treatise never could.

I've put together a collection of some of my favorite quotes that I hope will inspire you in writing your legacy statement. Read through them. There's a good chance that one of them will strike a chord with you. Don't hesitate to incorporate a quote in your legacy statement. It can be a great way to pass on the same feelings you had when you first read it.

I'll start with a quote from Harriet Beecher Stow, author of **Uncle Tom's Cabin**, that I believe captures the motive behind many legacy statements.

"The bitterest tears shed over graves are for words left unsaid and deeds left undone."

The power of this statement is unmistakable. What better reason for creating a legacy statement than to erase the specter of "words left unsaid?" Ms. Stowe then continues:

"She never knew how I loved her. He never knew what he was to me. I always meant to make more of our friendship. I did not know what he was to me until he was gone. Such words are the poisoned arrows which cruel Death shoots backward at us from the door of the sepulcher.

"How much more we might make of our family life, of our friendships, if every secret thought of love blossomed into a deed! We are not now speaking merely of personal caresses. These may or may not be the best language of affection. Many are endowed with a delicacy, a fastidiousness of physical organization, which shrinks away from too much of these, repelled and overpowered. But there are words and looks and little observances, thoughtfulnesses, watchful little attentions, which speak of love, which make it

manifest, and there is scarce a family that might not be richer in heart-wealth for more of them."
                        - Harriet Beecher Stowe

Leaving a legacy through a Legacy Statement and, as we will see later in this course, through charitable actions and giving, is our attempt at immortality – to leave a part of us behind.

Two quotes from William Shakespeare express this desire.

"There is a history in all men's lives."
                        - William Shakespeare

"I have immortal longings in me."
                        - William Shakespeare

As does this statement by Albert Camus:

"If, after all, men cannot always make history have meaning, they can always act so that their own lives have one."
                        - Albert Camus

Leaving a legacy is more than leaving money and possessions to our heirs. We realize there are other things of great value that we can pass on.

"A man's life does not consist in the abundance of his possessions"
                        - Jesus (Luke 12:15)

"It is through creating, not possessing, that life is revealed.
- Vida D. Scudder

One purpose of a Legacy Statement is to give advice and impart wisdom to your loved ones.

"I have found the best way to give advice to your children is to find out what they want and then advise them to do it.
- Harry S Truman

"When we see men of worth, we should think of equaling them; when we see men of a contrary character, we should turn inwards and examine ourselves."
- Confucious

"To know the road ahead, ask those coming back."
- Chinese Proverb

"Write down the advice of him who loves you, though you like it not at present."
- English Proverb

"Happiness comes of the capacity to feel deeply, to enjoy simply, to think freely, to risk life, to be needed."
- Storm Jameson

The expression of charity and the gifts of philanthropy have resulted in some of the most beautiful and meaningful quotes ever written.

"You must give some time to your fellow men. Even if it's a little thing, do something for others — something for which you get no pay but the privilege of doing it."
- Albert Schweitzer

"Sometimes when we are generous in small, barely detectable ways it can change someone else's life forever."
- Margaret Cho

"I am a little pencil in the hand of a writing God who is sending a love letter to the world."
- Mother Teresa

"We make a living by what we get, we make a life by what we give."
- Winston Churchill

"Many persons have a wrong idea of what constitutes true happiness. It is not attained through self-gratification but through fidelity to a worthy purpose."
- Helen Keller

"At the end of your life, you will never regret not having passed one more test, not winning one more verdict, or not closing one more deal. You will regret

time not spent with a husband, a friend, a child, or a parent.”
- Barbara Bush

“Life's greatest happiness is to be convinced we are loved.”
- Victor Hugo

“What we have done for ourselves alone dies with us. What we have done for others and the world remains, and is immortal.”
- Albert Pike

“A human being is part of a whole, called by us the Universe, a part limited in time and space. He experiences himself, his thoughts and feelings, as something separated from the rest a kind of optical delusion of his consciousness. This delusion is a kind of prison for us, restricting us to our personal desires and to affection for a few persons nearest us. Our task must be to free ourselves from this prison by widening our circles of compassion to embrace all living creatures and the whole of nature in its beauty.”
- Albert Einstein

STEP FOUR:

DEVELOP AN OUTLINE

Now is the time to coordinate your themes into an outline. Your outline helps you organize your thoughts. It is a blueprint you will use to build your Legacy Statement.

Some tips to help you develop your outline:

1.   Work from your Purpose.   State the Purpose you identified in Step Two as clearly and with as much detail as possible. You will consistently refer to this during the development of your outline.

2.   Review the paragraphs you wrote during the exercise in Step Three. Determine if and how each paragraph relates to your Purpose. With that in mind, write a one-sentence summary of each paragraph that relates to your Purpose.

3.   Organize your summary sentences.   In doing so, you should strive to have your outline fulfill these functions:

    •   support your Purpose.

    •   establish the order and relationships of your themes and exercise paragraphs.

- clarify the relationship between your purpose and themes.

There are different approaches to organizing your outline. Your message may be better expressed using one of these methods over another:

Problem Solution. In this model you will identify a problem, issue or objective. It will be your main point. Your subpoints would then address the issue, developing a solution. These subpoints will frequently be the exercise summary sentences. An example is as follows:

    I.   Problem, Issue or Objective

        A.   Solution - Exercise Summary Sentence
        B.   Solution - Another Exercise Summary Sentence

    II.   Second Problem, Issue or Objective

        A.   Solution - Exercise Summary Sentence
        B.   Solution - Exercise Summary Sentence

Cause and Effect. You can state events as the main point and use your exercise summary sentences to show the effects caused by such events. Example:

I. Started the Family Business

    A.   Instilled a sense of responsibility and work ethic in me

    B.   Taught me to think outside-of-the-box.

Chronological. You can recite events in their chronological order to express your message. Example:

I. Started the Family Business

    A.   Lost my previous job and needed to find a way to support my family.

        1.   Instilled a sense of responsibility

        2.   Taught me to be creative - list examples

    A well-written outline will serve to organize your thoughts, feelings and ideas into a coherent and flowing structure. If at all possible, you should prepare your outline in a word processing program such as Microsoft Word. This will make it easy to edit, reorganize or re-write the outline.

STEP FIVE

PREPARE A DRAFT

If you look back to Step Four, you will recall that your outline is the blueprint for your Legacy Statement. Just as a builder uses blueprints and plans to construct a house, your outline will be the foundation of your first draft.

Starting with your outline, you can begin to fill in the full paragraphs from the writing prompts exercise that correspond with each summary sentence in your outline. Again, a word processor makes this a simple task.

If you are writing without using the writing prompts exercise, you can begin to draft paragraphs that expound on your outline topics.

If your outline is complete, you can start anywhere you wish. You don't have to write from start to finish. This can help you overcome writer's block. If you are drawing a blank with one topic, simply move to the next and begin writing.

Keep in mind that this is only a first draft. It doesn't need to read perfectly at this point. The most important thing is to get all of the material on paper. You can add, delete, and revise later.

STEP SIX

REVISE AND EDIT

Now that you have completed your first draft, the next step is to revise your Legacy Statement. Before going any further, we should discuss exactly what the term, "revise," means.

Revising the Legacy Statement is not editing the paper. The time to correct grammar, punctuation, and other technical matters is after you have revised the content. Editing is the fine-tuning stage of the writing. What I am talking about by revising is to look at your legacy statement from a fresh perspective.

The first step in revising is to read your Legacy Statement aloud. You can better hear weaknesses in writing than you can see them. While reading your first draft aloud, you should consider the following:

- Does the first draft clearly address the purpose for which I am writing the Legacy Statement?

- Is the emotional tone I use appropriate for my audience and purpose?

- Does my theme adequately express the purpose I have chosen?

- What more could I say in the next draft?

- What could I eliminate in the next draft? Have I used irrelevant ideas? Have I been repetitive?

Before starting the revision process, I would recommend that you take some time off after writing the first draft. You can use this time to completely forget about the project, or to reflect on your target audience and purpose. This allows you to step back from the Legacy Statement and develop a fresh perspective. It may generate new ideas and approaches that you can incorporate into your Legacy Statement.

During the revision stage, you will need to re-read your draft a number of times. Try to read from different angles each time. For example, put yourself in the place of your target audience for one of the readings. Imagine what that person's reaction would be. Will your draft achieve the intended result?

On another reading, concentrate on whether your theme is the proper approach to achieve your purpose.

Still another reading - ask yourself: does this sound like me? Does this statement sound like my core beliefs and my values?

By reading your drafts aloud and reflecting on considerations mentioned above, you will be surprised how readily you will discover necessary revisions.

Once you have re-written your drafts so that you are satisfied with its content, it is time to edit your Legacy Statement.

The first thing to do is check for spelling errors. If you are using a word processing program, you should run spell check on it. This does not eliminate the need for you to check spelling visually. Some mistakes and misspellings actually form other words, so your spell check program will not pick them up.

Next, correct grammatical or punctuation errors. When this is done, re-read your Legacy Statement again to find revision and editing items you may have missed.

Congratulations, your hard work and diligence have paid off. You have created a gift for your loved ones that they will treasure for years.

MOTIVATION AND PROCRASTINATION.

I'm not going to lie to you, writing a Legacy Statement is hard work.

I've tried to create a system to guide you through the process with step-by-step procedures, legacy writing exercises and writing prompts, with the idea that dividing the work into smaller chunks will make it less imposing and more manageable. Still, it will be easy to put this project off until tomorrow – if you allow yourself.

Procrastination is a nasty little habit because it can be rationalized so easily. You convince yourself that you will start working on your legacy statement as soon as some other project is finished. Like cleaning your closet, paying your bills or washing the dog. You're not giving up on writing your legacy statement, you're just going to start tomorrow.

The basis of procrastination can usually be narrowed down to two reasons:

1. The perceived need to finish other projects. There is always something else that needs to be done. Unless you make a firm decision that writing your legacy statement is a worthwhile project that takes priority over the other projects, you will never get started. Or, if you do get started, you will never finish.

2. An obsession with perfection. Some people will not start a project until they believe that they have everything perfect. If you need to have a perfect setting in which to write, if the mood needs to be perfect, if you still need to do some more research before starting, or if you're worried that you won't be able to create a perfect finished product, chances are you will never get started. Remember, nobody's first draft is perfect. And every great manuscript started with the author sitting down and writing the first word.

Mark Twain was a writer who dealt with procrastination and had to conquer it each time he wrote. His method for doing so is captured in his quote, *"The secret of getting ahead is getting started. The secret of getting started is breaking your complex overwhelming tasks into small manageable tasks, and then starting on the first one."*

The best way to overcome this resistance is to hold yourself accountable or, better yet, to tell a good friend or family member about your Legacy Statement project and have him or her hold you accountable. Procrastination is a condition that is too easy to fall back into without the conviction to get through it and the help of someone else to push you.

You have to set aside a time each day to work on your Legacy Statement and force yourself to adhere to that schedule no matter what other projects present themselves. And you have to be held strictly accountable. Sit down every day at the same time and write. Anything. Answer the writing prompts. Work on the legacy writing exercises. Re-write something you drafted yesterday. Just write.

The popular English writer, Somerset Maugham, was once asked if he wrote on a schedule or only when struck by inspiration. His reply, "I write only when inspiration strikes. Fortunately, it strikes every morning at nine o'clock sharp."

LESSON THREE:

THE FAMILY BUSINESS LEGACY STATEMENT

Family businesses have been the backbone of America's small business since this country was founded. By some estimates, over 90% of American businesses are family owned.

However, a disturbing fact is that less than 33% of all family businesses survive into the second generation. It gets even worse each generation that follows.

While there are a number of reasons for this unfortunate trend, one is the lack of preparation for children to understand, value, and operate the business. Many children simply don't have an understanding and appreciation of the basis and evolution of the family business.

The ideals, strategies, and experience of creating and growing the enterprise don't pass to the next generation as easy as the shares of stock. As a result, the business loses its focus. Procedures that took years of trial and error to perfect are abandoned. Customers begin to sense a change in the business - and not for the better. Performance begins to slide. New procedures are instituted to try to remedy the situation, usually moving the company farther from the ideals and practices that made it successful. The decline continues and eventually the family business is out of business.

One way to prevent this scenario is for the owner of the business to engage in proper business succession planning. Similar to estate planning, most people think of succession planning as the legal procedure to transfer ownership and operation of the business. They think of buy-sell agreements, key man life insurance, and stock pledge agreements. These are extremely important. In fact, they are essential. But a business succession plan that deals only with the legal aspects is woefully incomplete.

In addition to the transfer of ownership and control, there must be a transfer of the values, ideals, culture, and traditions of the business. This is the role of the Family Business Legacy Statement. But it would be a mistake to wait until the time of transfer to address these issues. The preparation and training of family members to take over the business should begin before any transition is pending.

Succession Planning for your business needs to commence years before the transition takes place. In many instances, the family members do not want to take control of the business. Only through early succession planning can this be discovered and a proper successor named and developed.

Early considerations for your family successor are encouraging them to obtain the proper education and degrees, working in non-management aspects of the business to gain experience and perspective, and mentoring them to learn not only the business but life lessons as well.

A written business succession plan should be drafted and discussed with the successors. It should address, at a minimum, the structure of the business, financial aspects of both the business and the transition, succession strategies, management continuity, successor training, and family dynamics.

The Family Business Legacy Statement should be a supplement to the business succession plan and the legal documents.

In writing the Family Business Legacy Statement, the same steps we went through for the Legacy Statement apply - only your purpose is to assist in your family business succession.

Some possible themes and issues to address are as follows:

1. Determine your family's core values as they relate to the business. Answering questions such as:

- Why was the business started? What needs were met by starting the business?

- Why do your customers/clients select your business's services or products as opposed to all the choices available to them?

- What challenges have you overcome, and what qualities or beliefs helped you succeed?

- Who was the most influential person in your business career, and why?

- How do you envision the future of the company?

2. Develop a vision statement for the family business. This is a description of the purposes of the business. Why was it started? What were the initial goals of the business? How have they changed over time, and why? What are the most important qualities you envision the business embodying?

3. Acknowledge and consider the differences between you and other family members. Between different family members. Your successors may not have the same passions that you did. They may not

understand the experiences you gained while starting and building the business. Each family member has a different style, temperament, and drive which can lead to disagreements and conflict. You need to consider these issues and more when advising your successors.

4. Recount the story of the business. Articulate the history and family heritage and explain how that affected the creation and development of the business. Try to capture the philosophies and the emotions. The story of the family business does more to involve your family in its culture and ideals than anything else.

5. Acknowledge and understand the family's problems and issues. No matter how hard you or your successors try to separate business from family, it will always play a role in the success of the business. Many family businesses fail, not because of business or financial reasons, but because of unresolved family issues that eat away at the integrity of the business.

6. Recognize and describe the potential pitfalls and challenges the business will face. Provide insight as to possible solutions, the mindset needed to face these challenges, and past successes and failures in confronting them.

7. Endorse advisors and confidants that your successors can turn to and rely on. Experienced and knowledgeable persons with expertise can provide a different perspective and discourage possible family feuds.

Whether a family can preserve its wealth from generation to generation is based in a large part on its system of governance. In order for this system to be strong enough to endure, it must be founded on a set of shared values that express the family's uniqueness.

These values must remain relevant as they are passed from generation to generation. The issue of succession, on both a family level and business level, is critical to the long term viability of the business and the family's wealth.

To put it another way, each successive generation must "buy into" the values, ideals, and uniqueness of the family. There needs to be an enduring cohesiveness in the bloodline.

One very powerful way to preserve the values, traditions, and ideals that foster this uniqueness is through a Legacy Statement or Family Business Legacy Statement.

LESSON FOUR:

LEAVING A LEGACY TO YOUR COMMUNITY

Ruth's husband of 53 years recently passed away. In their years together, Ruth and Sam had raised three children. All three are now married with their own children, live across the country from Ruth, and are financially successful.

In fact, Ruth and Sam had accumulated quite a large estate. Sam was a senior manager for a manufacturing company and had started working for the company almost from its inception. In the early days, when cash flow was short, the company rewarded Sam with stock ownership. Each year, instead of a monetary bonus, Sam would receive more shares of stock. By the time he retired at the age of 65, Sam's shares in the company were worth over $3 million.

Ruth and Sam lived comfortably but not extravagantly. Much of the happiness in their lives was derived from the companionship of their time together. When Sam died, it left a huge void in Ruth's life.

In order to help adjust to her new circumstances, Ruth began contemplating how she would spend her time and make her life fulfilling. Examining her values and beliefs, Ruth recalled that she and Sam had always placed a high value on education. Neither of them had attended college, and they wanted to make sure that didn't hold back their children.

Even before the company stock increased in value, Ruth and Sam set aside money that would eventually pay for their children's education. As a result, all three of their children earned graduate degrees which helped lead to extremely successful careers.

Ruth decided that she wanted to honor Sam's life and, at the same time, provide educational opportunities to those in her community that might otherwise not be able to afford it.

In reviewing her situation, Ruth saw that she had more money than she would ever be able to spend. Her children were financially secure and did not need an inheritance. After consulting with her children and financial advisor, Ruth decided to create an educational fund that provided scholarships each year to students who met certain qualifications.

Each year, Ruth and her children would get together for a family gathering. They would review applications from scholarship candidates and select those that met the criteria they had established. Ruth and her children planned that the grandchildren would participate in this process when they were old enough. In fact, Ruth hoped this would become a family tradition, passed on from generation to generation.

To ensure this tradition, Ruth prepared a Legacy Statement. She filled it with memories of her life together with Sam, the values that the two of them shared and a request to the future generations of her family that they continue to honor those values by maintaining the educational fund she had created.

She knew Sam would have been pleased. By this selfless act of charity, Ruth ensured that Sam's and her legacy would impact their community for years to come.

Many people feel compelled to give back to their community. After all, what better way is there to leave your legacy than by helping others? A plan of charitable giving is the action behind the words of the Legacy Statement.

There are causes near and dear to each of our hearts that we have a desire to support. Unfortunately, many people don't know how to set up a charitable plan. Even more unfortunate, many don't believe they have the resources to contribute to charity.

In this course, I will show you different ways to set up a charitable program. How to create a vehicle that will allow you to give to the cause of your choice, on your terms, for generations to come. How even smaller estates can create a charitable legacy that will positively impact lives. How you can reduce and eliminate estate taxes through charitable giving. How you can give a large portion of your estate to charity and still have your heirs receive a larger inheritance than if you had not given.

If you have a large estate, you are going to be a philanthropist whether you plan for it or not. If you make no charitable plan of your own, your default charity will be the United States Treasury.

Estate taxes are levied at the federal and state levels and confiscate a significant percentage of all estates that exceed the maximum estate tax credit. Some high net worth individuals have engaged in estate planning to be able to pass the maximum amount allowed by law to their heirs. But in a lot of cases, part of the estate is still subject to estate taxes. For these taxpayers, their legacy is contributing to the programs and operations of the government.

Think about it. Do you believe the government is doing a good job of applying our tax money? Or do you think you can make better decisions on how your money is used?

What a lot of people don't know is that their charity doesn't have to be the government. You can control that part of your estate that is earmarked to go to the government in the form of estate taxes.

On average, the government spends $85,000 per second. How much of an impact do you think your estate tax contribution will make to society? And what will it support? Will it be a program or cause that you feel strongly about, or will it be used in a way that does not represent your values? Remember, sharing your legacy is about passing on your values.

Fortunately, the government has provided us with certain credits and deductions to apply against our estate tax liability. The most powerful of these is the charitable deduction. Any portion of your estate that you contribute to a qualified charity is not counted as a portion of your estate that is subject to estate taxation. In addition, charitable contributions provide deductions that will reduce your income tax liability. You will see later in this course how the charitable deduction can be used to actually increase the size of your estate.

But you're thinking, "this is not supposed to be about estate taxes and tax planning. This is supposed to tell me how I can leave a legacy."

And leaving a legacy is what we will concentrate on. However, the concepts regarding the tax benefits of charitable planning are so powerful, they can greatly increase the scope and impact of your legacy. So I ask you to bear with me. I'll do my best not to get us bogged down in legalese and the tax code. What I will discuss will be general outlines - all with the intent of improving and enhancing your legacy. You should contact a tax planning accountant or estate planning attorney for more in-depth information and to implement your charitable plan.

THE CONCEPT OF SOCIAL CAPITAL

In the first part of this section about leaving a legacy to your community, I talked about the portion of your estate that would be swallowed up by estate taxes. This part of your estate is known as your *social capital*. It is that portion of your estate that you cannot pass on to your heirs, that instead is paid in taxes.

Most estate planning deals with that portion of your estate that you can pass to your heirs - your *personal capital*. Effective estate plans can reduce the amount of your *social capital* so that you can leave more to your heirs. But, very few plans focus directly on the *social capital*. This is unfortunate because much of your charitable legacy comes from your *social capital*.

By creating a legacy plan that focuses on your *social capital*, you can:

1. increase the amount you pass on to your heirs;
2. improve your current financial condition;
3. make sure all of your social capital goes to causes you select, and
4. leave a legacy that will impact your community for generations.

DEFINING YOUR CHARITABLE INTENT

Many people have a cause that they are passionate about. This is the first step in your community legacy plan: to define your charitable intent.

I've worked with clients who feel a strong desire to give back to their community, but have trouble deciding how. They are unable to pinpoint a certain area they wish to benefit.

A lot of the time, passion is aroused by people you admired in the past. You may have known someone who bravely battled a disease and you may be inspired to help others in the same situation. You may have been affected by the determination of a person who overcame obstacles to acquire an education. You may be influenced by the work of others who have strived to discover means to solve social conditions or otherwise help society.

Our world is such that there is an abundance of causes all needing help and support. The library and bookstores are full of biographies of philanthropists, inspirational figures, and leaders of movements and causes.

There are lists of charitable organizations in print and online. These lists provide descriptions of the purpose of the organization and usually refer you to other sources about the cause.

I will speak more about Community Foundations later in this course, but for now search to see if there is one in your area. These organizations can provide you with valuable information about the needs of the community and their staff can counsel you to help identify a cause.

Discuss the issue with family, friends, and colleagues. Find out what others are passionate about and why. All of these exercises will help give you an insight into what causes appeal to you.

The cause you choose does not have to be "charitable" as defined by the Federal Tax Code. However, legally recognized charities provide more planning options. Most of the strategies we discuss later involve tax benefits only available with charitable contributions recognized by the IRS.

Once you decide to use your financial estate and social capital to create a legacy to your community, your next step is to decide the vehicle you will use to provide the benefits.

There are many factors to consider when choosing the vehicle.

- How much social capital do you wish to use?

- How will this fit in with your traditional family estate plan?

- Do you want the contribution made during your lifetime, after your death, or both?

- What tax benefits are available for your plan?

This section will describe different alternatives for creating your legacy and apply these and other questions to help determine which is best for your situation.

Before we get started - **a word of warning**. This is not a do-it-yourself project. You should assemble and work with a team to get this done. In addition to you and your family, team members should include your financial advisor, a CPA or tax advisor familiar with charitable issues, and an estate planning attorney.

After finishing this course, you should have the knowledge and perspective to quarterback your team, making the major decisions and delegating the implementation to your other team members.

LESSON FIVE:

THE FAMILY FOUNDATION

An increasing number of people are using Family Foundations to carry out their legacy plans. The publicity surrounding the Bill and Melinda Gates Trust has caused people to explore this alternative.

A Family Foundation is a form of private foundation. It is a separate legal entity (usually a trust or non -profit corporation) that is managed by a board consisting of the founder's family members, friends and colleagues.

The Family Foundation has the following benefits and features:

1. Supports charitable organizations determined by the board.

2. Provides an income tax deduction to those who contribute to it.

3. Minimizes your estate tax liability.

4. Avoids capital gains tax on any appreciated asset contributed to the foundation.

5. Allows you to create and manage the Family Foundation's investment strategy.

6. Empowers your children and descendants within the community and provides continuing employment for them.

7. Preserves your family's and your legacy for generations to come.

Supports Charitable Organizations

Your Family Foundation will make contributions to charitable causes and organizations each year. Most families make their contributions in the form of grants to qualifying domestic organizations such as the United Way; however, some foundations are structured to directly fund exempt charitable operations. These are called operating foundations. One of the benefits of a Family Foundation is that you will be able to select the recipients of your charitable distributions each year.

Provides an Income Tax Deduction

If you contribute cash to a non-operating Family Foundation, you can receive an income tax deduction in the year of the gift. The amount of the deduction you claim can be up to 30 percent of your adjusted gross income in the year of contribution. Donations in excess of this limit can be carried forward for 5 years. If your gift is made with assets other than cash (stocks, real estate), you can claim a deduction up to 20 percent. If you donate appreciated stock that you have owned for at least one year, the income tax deduction will be based on the fair market value of the stock.

As an example, if your adjusted gross income is $100,000, and you make a $50,000 cash contribution to your Family Foundation, you can deduct only $30,000 in the year of the contribution and carry over the remaining $20,000 for up to 5 years.

If you give stock or real estate that you have owned for more than a year, and your adjusted gross income is $100,000, you can only deduct $20,000 in the year of the gift.

Minimizes Your Estate Tax Liability.

You have the option of contributing to your Family Foundation during your lifetime or after your death through your will, trust, life insurance or other beneficiary designations. Any property you leave to a qualifying charity at the time of your death is deductible 100 percent from your gross estate for estate tax purposes. Further, any contributions you make to your Family Foundation during your lifetime will not reduce your annual gift tax exclusion or your lifetime gift tax credit.

For purposes of estate tax deductions, the Family Foundation is considered a qualifying charity, the same as any public charity. Therefore, you can leave your entire estate to your Family Foundation and receive a charitable deduction for all of it. This would totally eliminate your estate tax liability.

Later we will discuss how you can do this and still leave an inheritance for your children and, at the same time, provide an income for you and your spouse.

Avoids Capital Gains on Appreciated Assets

If you own stocks, real estate, or other assets that have greatly increased in value, and you are reluctant to dispose of them because you wish to avoid the capital gains taxes, you can transfer the assets to your Family Foundation without any capital gains liability. The

Family Foundation can then sell the assets and, because it is a charitable entity, not be liable for any capital gains taxes.

Allows You to Create and Manage the Investment Strategy

The board of the Family Foundation is responsible for managing its finances and assets. While this duty can be delegated to professional advisors, you will retain control over those decisions.

Empowers Your Children and Provides Continuing Employment for Them

A Family Foundation can maintain your legacy into perpetuity. It is an effective means of involving your children and future generations in that legacy. Many families create Family Foundations for the purpose of involving their family in their philanthropic efforts. It becomes an excellent way to teach children about the family values, responsibility, and managing money.

Family members are usually members of the board of the Family Foundation. Provisions can be made to enable future generations to succeed them. The board can direct the administration of the Family Foundation and can direct the charitable distributions. They can receive a reasonable salary for their service and reimbursement for all expenses they incur while performing their duties.

Their activities within the Family Foundation also provide a certain measure of empowerment in the community which continues the family's significance and legacy.

Preserves the Family Legacy

Because a Family Foundation can exist into perpetuity, you and your family can remain a valuable influence to your community long after you are gone. It is an ideal method for you to bequeath your values and ideals of philanthropy and social responsibility to your descendants for generations to come.

IS A FAMILY FOUNDATION RIGHT FOR YOU?

As we just saw, a Family Foundation is a valuable method to create and maintain your legacy and, at the same time, enhance tax benefits and estate planning goals. But a Family Foundation is not for everyone. This section discusses considerations you should make before deciding whether or not to create a Family Foundation.

1. Is my estate large enough to consider a Family Foundation?

While there is no set threshold for establishing a Family Foundation, your estate, particularly the *social capital* portion, should be large enough to warrant the start up and administration costs while still making relevant gifts.

Many tax specialists recommend that your estate have at least $500,000 of *social capital* to obtain enough tax benefits to justify the expenses. That means $500,000 that would otherwise be subject to estate taxes. Also, most Family Foundations are set up as endowments. All charitable contributions and administrative expenses are paid out of the income generated by the Family Foundation. The principal is never touched. As a result, the assets held in the Family Foundation will have to generate enough income each year to pay legal and accounting fees, board members' salaries, and other administrative expenses, as well as make a significant gift to your selected charities.

A typical method that Family Foundations use to pay their board members is to apply the difference between the total income and the required charitable distributions. For example, if your Family Foundation of $500,000 earns 10 percent on its assets, and the Foundation documents call for payment of 5 percent of the value of the assets to charities, the difference would be available for administrative expenses.

Principal Amount of Fund	5% Payout	% Earnings	Earnings for Year	Available for Expenses
$500,000	$25,000	10%	$50,000	$25,000

If, in a particular year, the Family Foundation's assets only earn 6%, only 1% would be available for expenses.

Principal Amount of Fund	5% Payout	% Earnings	Earnings for Year	Available for Expenses
$500,000	$25,000	6%	$30,000	$5,000

Because of the increased popularity of the Family Foundation, administrative expenses have gone down. New companies have formed in response to the demand that provide administration services to Family Foundations. Because these companies have systems and expertise on hand, they can leverage their talent and work with many foundations, thereby reducing the cost. They also relieve you, your family and other Board members of the risks of not complying with the tax laws.

2. How much time do you have to devote to the administration of your Family Foundation?

Even if you hire an administration company, you will have to oversee the operations of your Family

Foundation. Part of the advantages of setting up a Family Foundation is the ability to maintain control over investment and grant decisions.

Like your own investments, you and the board members of your family foundation will need to develop an investment strategy for its asset portfolio.

You will also have the duty, along with the other board members, of reviewing grant requests and making grants from the Family Foundation. This is usually done on an annual or more frequent basis.

You will also oversee the reporting and record keeping required by law. The IRS has strict rules and regulations for private foundations and the board has a fiduciary duty to make sure they are complied with.

In summary, Family Foundations give you the most control over your charitable giving plan and legacy. It is the best way to involve future generations. However, it is the most expensive and time consuming of all the charitable giving alternatives.

CREATING YOUR FAMILY FOUNDATION.

Now you know what a Family Foundation is and how it can help create a legacy for you and your family. You have considered the pros and cons and have decided to move forward. This section gives you a step by step process to create your Family Foundation.

STEP ONE:

DEVELOP A GIVING STRATEGY.

Before you roll up your sleeves and start the creation process, you must decide what it is you want to accomplish. Your giving strategy is a set of goals and objectives specifying the purposes, amounts, timing and manner in which your family will make its charitable contributions.

The following exercise is the most important part of formulating a giving strategy:

<u>Write a Family Mission Statement</u>. Each member of the family should write down his or her ideas and priorities regarding giving. What organizations and causes does he or she want to support? Why? How will the gifts be made? How does this support the family legacy? Then they should hold a family meeting to discuss these ideas and hammer out the family mission statement.

This meeting should not be taken lightly. Each family member should set aside the time, free from interruption, to participate. The meeting should have an agenda, and the goal of creating a family mission statement should be understood by all family members.

At the meeting, each person's list of ideas and priorities should be read and discussed. Those common to more than one family member should be noted. Competing ideas and goals should be discussed and prioritized. At the conclusion of the meeting, your family should have selected the top goals and incorporated them into a mission statement. The basic procedure for writing a family mission statement is similar to that of the Legacy Statement. You should review the steps from that section, paying special attention to the writing prompts questions entitled "SERVING OTHERS."

STEP TWO:

CREATE AND STRUCTURE THE FAMILY FOUNDATION.

Now that you have a family mission statement, you need to formalize the Family Foundation. A Family Foundation generally takes one of two forms: a nonprofit corporation or a trust.

Each type of entity has its advantages and disadvantages as shown by the comparison chart on the next page.

ISSUE	NON-PROFIT CORP.	TRUST
Creation of Entity	Requires filing of Articles of Incorporation with the state.	Declaration of Trust does not need to be filed.
Annual Fees	Must file Annual Report and pay annual fee.	No reports or fees.
Revision Documents	Amendment of Article of Incorporation and Bylaws is simple procedure.	Some states require court action to revise Declaration of Trust.
Liability of Board Members	Corporate directors may have more insulation from liability	Trustees are usually more involved in operations and subject to more liability.
Obtaining Tax Exempt Status	Both entities are required to	apply to the IRS

THE NONPROFIT CORPORATION

A nonprofit corporation is a legal entity created under the laws of the state in which it is formed. The corporation is created by preparing articles of incorporation and filing them with the state.

The Articles of Incorporation.

The articles of incorporation are required by state law to contain certain information such as the name of the corporation, the purpose and authorized activities of the corporation, and the duration. Every state has different requirements and an attorney experienced in corporate law should be retained.

1. The Corporation Name. Every state requires a corporation to have a name unique form all other corporations in the state. Most state governments have a web site where you can check for the availability of the name. Your name may recognize your family ("The Smith Family Foundation, Inc.) or your cause ("The North Florida Youth Foundation, Inc.").

2. Purpose. In order to comply with federal tax law, the stated purpose of the corporation must be a recognized charitable purpose. The charitable purpose that you state should reflect the values and conclusions of your family mission statement. The following language is generally used to state a charitable purpose:

> *Said corporation is organized exclusively for charitable, religious, educational and scientific purposes, including, for such purposes, the making of distributions to organizations that qualify as exempt organizations under Section 501(c)(3) of the Internal Revenue Code, or the corresponding section of any future federal tax code.*

The IRS also provides samples of provisions that apply to private foundations:

> *1. The corporation will distribute its income for each tax year at a time and in a manner as not to become subject to the tax on undistributed income imposed by section 4942 of the Internal Revenue Code, or the corresponding section of any future federal tax code.*
>
> *2. The corporation will not engage in any act of self-dealing as defined in Section 4941 of the Internal Revenue Code, or the corresponding section of any future federal tax code.*
>
> *3. The corporation will not retain any excess business holdings as defined in Section 4943(c) of the Internal Revenue Code, or the corresponding section of any future federal tax code.*

4.   The corporation will not make any investments in a manner as to subject it to tax under Section 4944 of the Internal Revenue Code, or the corresponding section of any future federal tax code.

5. The corporation will not make any taxable expenditures as defined in Section 4945(d) of the Internal Revenue Code, or the corresponding section of any future federal tax code.

3.   Initial Directors Names.   Many states require you to list the initial board of directors on the articles of incorporation.   These should be family members, friends, and trusted advisors who will make the decisions for your family foundations. Most states require listing an address.   Since this is public information, you should consider whether to use your home or office address.

You should be careful to review your state's laws on this matter. Many states require a minimum number of directors in nonprofit corporations.

It is a common practice to form the corporation with the minimum number of directors and increase that number through the years to add more family members as they become older.   The articles of incorporation can be amended on a regular basis to increase or decrease the number of directors.

4. Registered Agent and Address. The articles must also designate the name and address of a registered agent. This is the official contact person of the corporation. If suit is filed against a corporation, the summons may be effectively served on the corporation by delivering it to the registered agent at the registered address. Many corporations name their attorney as the registered agent, although any member or person who has a physical address (not a post office box) in the state of incorporation may be named.

The Bylaws.

The bylaws of a nonprofit corporation are a framework of regulations by which the corporation will operate.

Some examples of the issues the bylaws address are:

- Qualifications of members.

- Qualifications and election of directors. The bylaws provide requirements a person must meet to become a member of the board. It sets forth the mechanics of conducting an election of the board members, states how long a board member's term of service is, and tells how resigned or deceased board members are replaced.

- Meetings of the members and board. The bylaws outline the manner of giving notice and conducting these meetings. It also prescribes the number of required meetings each year and the frequency of those meetings.

- Description of the duties of the board and the officers.

- Process for amending the bylaws.

- Regulation of fiscal matters.

The bylaws are not recorded with the state; however, they must be submitted with the corporation's application to be treated as a charitable organization under federal tax law. As a result, care must be taken in drafting them.

Organizational Minutes and Meeting.

The board must meet pursuant to the requirements of the bylaws to perform certain organizational duties. These duties include election or appointment of the officers. Most state laws provide that nonprofit corporations can act through their officers (President, Vice President, Secretary, and Treasurer are examples). Any document binding the non-profit corporation must be signed by a duly elected and authorized officer. The organizational meeting also authorizes the creation of banking and investment accounts. The decision reached in this meeting are documented in minutes of the meeting which, in many instances, are required to show evidence of authority.

The organizational minutes, as well as minutes of all subsequent corporate meetings, should be kept by the Secretary and made available pursuant to state law.

THE FOUNDATION TRUST

Another entity commonly used to form a Family Foundation is a trust. This was historically the traditional method; however, nonprofit corporations have become very popular today.

There are two types of trusts that are used to create Family Foundations. The first is an *inter vivos trust*, or a trust created during a person's lifetime. The second type, a *testamentary trust*, is created after a person's death by that person's Will. In this course, we will mainly be discussing inter vivos trusts.

In an inter vivos trust, the organizational document is known as the *declaration of trust*. While the choice between a trust and nonprofit corporation is generally one of personal choice, there are some advantages to organizing as a trust.

Some states have fewer regulations and requirements for trusts under state law than corporations. While all articles of incorporation are required to be filed with the state, many states do not require filing of declarations of trust. Likewise, many states don't require annual reporting and fees for trusts and they do for nonprofit corporations. As a result, the board members are not disclosed, giving more privacy to the trust.

Most states require a minimum number of board members or directors in a nonprofit corporation. A Family Foundation in trust form may need only one person to serve as trustee.

Basics of the Trust Form.

A trust is an arrangement under which a person holds and manages property (the "Trustee") contributed by another person (the "Grantor" or "Donor") for the benefit of a third person or persons (the "Beneficiaries").

In the case of the Family Foundation, you are the Grantor. You have created the trust and have made the initial contributions to it. You may also set it up so that you are the Trustee or you can have a "Board of Trustees" who will manage and distribute the trust property. The Beneficiaries are those persons or organizations to whom you ultimately distribute the earnings from the property.

The Declaration of Trust usually performs the same roles that the articles of incorporation and bylaws perform for the nonprofit corporation. It creates the entity and provides a framework of regulations under which the Trustee or Board of Trustees will manage, invest, and distribute the trust property.

STEP THREE:

OBTAIN AN EMPLOYER IDENTIFICATION NUMBER

The Employer Identification Number to the Family Foundation is like a Social Security Number to an individual. Whether you select a trust or nonprofit corporation as your entity, you will need to apply for an Employer Identification Number (EIN).

To obtain an EIN, you must complete IRS Form SS-4, "Application for an Employer Identification Number." You can find this form on the IRS website (www.irs.gov). Follow the links from the home page to Forms and Publications. You can also apply online. I would suggest printing the Form SS-4 first, filling in the information by hand, and then typing it into the online application. The IRS will usually give you the number immediately.

STEP FOUR:

OBTAIN YOUR CHARITABLE EXEMPTION

In order to have a tax exempt status and for contributions to your Family Foundation to be deductible as charitable contributions, you next need to file an application for tax exemption with the IRS. Some states also require that you file a tax exemption application.

The proper form for applying for tax exempt status is IRS Form 1023 - "Application for Recognition of Exemption."

Completing Form 1023

Form 1023 is a cumbersome document that requires time and patience to complete. Also, there are some strategies that make it more likely that your entity will be accepted as tax exempt. For this reason, I advise that you retain an attorney or accountant who is familiar with this process to assist you.

Whether you retain professional assistance or try to tackle this form on your own, you will need to be familiar with the process. The following are materials and documents you should obtain before starting:

- a copy of Form 1023
- instructions for Form 1023 (IRS Publication)
- the Federal Employer Identification Number of the entity
- the organizational documents of the entity (if it is a nonprofit corporation - articles of incorporation and bylaws; if it is a trust - declaration of trust).
- names, addresses, and other information on the directors, officers, employees, and trustees of the entity.
- financial statements of the entity's operations.
- IRS Form 2848 - Power of Attorney and Declaration of Representative (to appoint an attorney, accountant, or someone other than a director, principal officer or trustee to represent the entity in matters related to the application).

The IRS has other publications to help you set up your Family Foundation. They include:

- IRS Publication 557 - Tax Exempt Status for your organization.
- IRS Publication 4420 - Applying for 501©)(3) Tax Exempt Status.

The IRS customer service hotline for exempt organizations is (877) 829-5500.

Timing of the Application.

You have 15 months from the effective date of organization of your entity to file Form 1023. For corporations, this would be the date of incorporation and for trusts, the date stated in the Declaration of Trust. You may request an additional 12 month extension.

If you file Form 1023 in a timely manner, the tax exempt status of the entity will be retroactive to the date of organization. This is important because it allows you to take advantage of the tax deductible nature of your initial contributions.

If you do not file the application within the required time, the tax exempt status of the entity is retroactive only to the date of filing the application.

Status While the Application is Pending.

It usually takes four to six months to receive a determination from the IRS whether it considers your entity to be tax exempt. In many instances, the IRS will request additional information to clarify relevant issues. This may delay the approval of the application. During the period while the IRS is making its determination, your entity may operate as a tax exempt organization.

OPERATING YOUR FAMILY FOUNDATION

Once you have set up your Family Foundation, you need to turn your attention to structuring its operation. This basically falls within five categories:

1. Corporate procedures and requirements.
2. Selection and responsibilities of the Board members.
3. Complying with legal and tax regulations.
4. Creating and implementing an investment strategy.
5. Selecting beneficiaries and making grants.

CORPORATE PROCEDURES AND REQUIREMENTS.

Whether your Family Foundation is organized as a nonprofit corporation or a trust, you will have certain requirements that must be met on an ongoing basis.

Corporations.

Most states require a corporation to file an annual report with an annual fee each year. The purpose of the report is to advise of any changes in officers, directors, and other aspects of the corporations. If the corporation fails to do this in a timely manner, there is usually a fee or penalty required to be paid. Some states even dissolve a corporation for failing to file its annual report.

Most states also require the members and the board of directors of a corporation to hold at least one meeting each year. The annual members' meeting usually provides the forum for the election of the board of directors, if provided for in the articles of incorporation or bylaws. Meetings of the board usually include election of successor board members (if provided for in the articles of incorporation or bylaws), appointment of officers, authorization of actions regarding banking, investing, and grant making.

All meetings should be recorded either electronically or in writing. All states have corporate records requirements to keep permanent minutes of meetings of members and the board of directors, and records of all actions taken by any committee of the board.

Trusts.

Every Family Foundation set up as a trust should keep minutes of meetings of the board of trustees.

Most states do not require trusts to be registered with the state. Trusts existing in any states that do require registration must comply with requirements regarding annual reports or notification of changes in status.

Some states require both corporations and trusts to file annual tax returns or financial statements. It is important that Family Foundations comply with these requirements so that they may maintain their tax exempt status.

SELECTION AND RESPONSIBILITY OF THE BOARD MEMBERS.

One of the most important considerations you will face when creating your Family Foundation involves the structure, election, and continuity of the Board.

You want to make sure that your Family Foundation continues to serve the charitable cause you have chosen. Since the Board makes all of the major decisions of the Family Foundation, each member and future member of the Board must be familiar with and understand the vision of the founder. This is one of the reasons it is so important to completely articulate you values, intentions, and goals in the Family Mission Statement.

Selection of the Initial Board.

As you will recall, the Board for a nonprofit corporation will consist of the board of directors as described in the bylaws. The Board for a trust will consist of a Board of Trustees as described in the Declaration of Trust.

The founder of a Family Foundation will usually wish to include himself or herself, family members, and close friends or trusted business associates.

While the documents spell out the goals and procedures of the Family Foundation, it is the Board that interprets these documents and ultimately makes the decisions that will shape the policy. Therefore, it is important that the initial Board members understand and agree to carry out the founder's intent.

Qualifications.

If your Family Foundation is to create a lasting legacy, it must continue to carry out its mission long after you are gone. Whether this happens is dependent on the future Board members. How can you, as the founder, ensure that your vision will continue? One way is to develop certain qualifications each new Board member must meet. These qualifications may require Board members to have achieved a certain educational level, have a certain occupation, or belong to certain organizations. You should strongly consider creating qualifications even for future family members.

Aside from the educational and occupational qualifications, you may wish to look at other intangible qualities.

1. Willingness to Participate. Every member chosen to serve on the Board should ideally be enthusiastic and motivated to do so. A Board member serving solely out of a sense of obligation will not exhibit the level of commitment needed to maintain the standards you have set. Not only will that person fail to put forth the effort you seek, they may also negatively affect the enthusiasm and commitment of other Board members.

If a prospective member does not share your enthusiasm, don't select them. If an existing member doesn't have the time or motivation to effectively contribute, they probably would rather not be saddled with the obligation of serving on the Board. Work out an arrangement to replace that person.

2. Objectivity. A good Board member should be able to objectively make decisions involving the management of the operations and the selection of grant recipients. Anyone who seeks to gain personally from his involvement or who has a conflict of interest should not be selected.

3. Experience. Every Board should consider at least one member who has experience in one or more of the aspects of the operation of the Family Foundation.

Number of Board Members.

Many states require the nonprofit corporations have at least three Board members. A trust can have as little as one trustee. While every Family Foundation must meet these legal requirements, you should take other factors into account when mandating the size of your board.

The primary consideration should be how many members the founder believes appropriate to manage the operations of the Family Foundation. Practical matters such as whether the Board will have only family members or allow outside members, the size of your family, and the amount of assets your Board will manage.

Provisions can be included in the bylaws or Declaration of Trust which will allow for changing the number of Board members. This may be appropriate if the amount of assets increases substantially in the future. Managing a Family Foundation and selecting grant recipients can become a time consuming job that may require delegation of those duties to a larger number of Board members as the Family Foundation grows.

Selection of Board Members.

Vacancies will occur in the Board as a result of death, resignation, or removal. It is important to develop a procedure to fill those vacancies.

The number one consideration in choosing a new Board member should be the perpetuation of the founder's intent. As we discussed in the previous section on qualifications, any candidate to fill a Board vacancy should understand and appreciate the founder's goals and values as set forth in the mission statement.

If the Family Foundation is organized as a nonprofit corporation, your state's law will have provisions relating to the selection or election of Board members. The procedures range from election by the members of the corporation to appointment by the remaining Board members. Many states allow this procedure to be dictated by the corporation's bylaws.

In the case of a trust entity, the provision for selecting successor trustees and Board members is dictated by the terms of the Declaration of Trust. Whatever procedure applies in your case, it is important that your Family Foundation be structured to preserve the original charitable intent.

Family Foundations are typically set up so that the founder and his or her descendants will have the authority to choose new Board members. This keeps control of the Foundation in the hands of the family and hopefully provides a better chance of maintaining the founder's original intent.

Even with control of the Family Foundation continuing in the family, it can be a challenge to make sure the founder's original mission is followed. For this reason, many families involve their children at early ages. They are encouraged to sit in on Board meetings to learn the mission of the Family Foundation and how it is carried out. Other family meetings can be held on a regular basis where the founder's intent can be discussed. If the founder wrote a Legacy Statement involving the charitable intent, it should be mandatory reading for young family members.

Every family should have a "story" where the charitable goals and ideals and how they originated are brought to life. This "story" should be a source of pride and center of tradition for the family. Quite often, this story will be told in the mission statement of the Family Foundation or the Founder's Legacy Statement.

Outside Board Members.

Most Family Foundations are family centered and a majority of the Board members comes from within the family. However, there are instances where it may be wise to choose members from outside the family.

Trusted advisors such as the family attorney, accountant, or financial advisors, may be good choices for Board members. Bringing professional advisors in can give the Board the expertise that family members may not have. There are stringent legal requirements and investment standards for Family Foundations. These outside Board members can help the family understand and comply with them in addition to bringing a different perspective to the Board.

Outside directors may also provide expertise in areas involving the Family Foundation's intent. For example, if the Foundation's focus is education or scholarships, then someone in that field can provide knowledge and perspective in making grants.

However you decide to structure the composition of the Board, the duties, qualifications, and manner of selection should be clearly stated in the bylaws or the Declaration of Trust. This will ensure that your Family Foundation will continue to operate and achieve the intent you envisioned for generations to come.

Removal of Board Members.

When setting up your Family Foundation, you will be working with the positive expectations and excitement of creating your legacy. Amid all of the optimism, it may not occur to you that some Board members may not be a good fit. For these cases, your documents should contain provisions for removal of Board members.

There are many standards for removal of a director that you should consider. Since the family is the core of the Family Foundation, you may wish to give family members a greater weight in deciding to remove a Board member. Or you may even wish to restrict this power to family members only.

In any case, this provision gives the family members a tool to ensure that the founder's original intent is followed.

Duties and Responsibility of Board Members.

Before agreeing to serve on the Board of a Family Foundation, a person will want to know what is required of them. The following is a list of duties and responsibilities of the typical Board members:

1. Maintaining the Founder's Intent. Each Board member is entrusted with determining, following, and maintaining the intent for which the founder created the Family Foundation. A well written Family Foundation Legacy Statement or Mission Statement will provide invaluable assistance.

Board members must define who the founder intended to help and how. Was it to provide educational opportunities to help disadvantaged students? Or was it more specific, restricting the assistance to those entering a certain profession? This intent may be stated in the organizational documents or in a Mission Statement or Legacy Statement composed by the founder.

Once the intent is determined, the Board is responsible for making sure this intent is carried out. In other words, their actions and decisions must reflect the intent of the founder. If the founder's intent was to make grants to organizations that are working to develop a cure for cancer, the Board has the duty not to award grants for other purposes.

Finally, the Board should periodically review the founder's intent and make sure it continues to remain relevant. A foundation that was created years ago to develop a cure for polio may have changed its mission to meet the circumstances now that polio has been effectively eradicated. Instead, it may now address its efforts on providing and administering vaccines to prevent the occurrence of the disease.

2. Selecting Recipients and Making Grants. The manner in which most Family Foundations achieve their mission is by making grants. The Board is entrusted with this duty. The decisions that the Board makes concerning who will receive grants and how they will be administered must reflect the intent of the founder and comply with state and federal law as well as the governing documents of the Family Foundation (the bylaws or the Declaration of Trust).

Many Family Foundations are set up as endowments. This means that the grants are made solely from the earnings of the foundation and the principal is not touched. The only exception to this standard is when it is necessary to invade the principal to meet the legal requirement that the Family Foundation distribute a minimum of 5% of its assets each fiscal year.

Other Family Foundations are created for a limited duration and the governing documents provide that the assets be distributed within a set number of years.

Typically, the Mission Statement of the Family Foundation creates a broad expression of intent. In that case, it is the role of the Board to establish qualification criteria for selecting grant recipients and a process for evaluating applications.

Once the Board has completed this step, the next step is to evaluate the potential grant recipients to make sure they meet the qualification criteria and comply with federal law.

If the Family Foundation is structured to make grants to other charitable organizations, the recipient organizations must be qualified public charities. This means they must be organized in strict compliance with Section 501(c)(3) of the Internal Revenue Code. If your Board is considering making a grant to an organization, you should request that the organization provide you with a copy of a letter from the IRS stating that it is recognized as a 501 (c)(3) organization.

The Board then makes a list of the potential recipients that meet the criteria established in the Mission Statement and refined by the Board. Additional information about these organizations can be obtained by reviewing its website, reading news articles about the organization, visiting the organization in person or by telephone, and talking with members of the community who have had experiences with the organization.

In evaluating potential grant recipients, most boards investigate many aspects of the organization. While these are not meant to be the only considerations, some areas they review are:

• **Purpose and Intent**. Does your potential grant recipient have a purpose that is complementary with that of your Family Foundation? This can be determined by review of the recipient's organizational documents and mission statement. Most charitable organizations make this information available online or provide a contact from whom to obtain it.

• **History.** Has the potential recipient made an impact in the area you are targeting? Has its mission been consistent over time? Most Family Foundations want to be assured that their contributions will be applied for the purpose and in the manner of the original intent. The track record of the recipient can be a powerful indication of this.

• **Leadership.** Who are the Board members and leaders of the potential grant recipient? Do they effectively represent the mission and ideals of the organization? Are they active in the community? An organization is typically defined by its leaders. No matter how attractive or well-aligned an organization's purpose is to your Family Foundation, if its Board cannot manifest these goals and ideals, your grant will not be effective. This is especially important for local or regional organizations where community involvement of the leaders can be the single largest impact of that organization.

EVALUATING THE IMPACT OF THE FAMILY FOUNDATION'S GRANTS.

The Board should constantly monitor the Family Foundation's grants to evaluate their impact. This evaluation leads to the consideration of the next year's grants. There are several aspects that the Board should consider:

1. Does the recipient organization use the grant for the purpose originally intended? Many charitable organizations change the focus or allocation of their work. Your Family Foundation may have chosen a particular recipient because of its emphasis on a certain cause. In future years, as the recipient's board evolves, it may place less emphasis on that cause. Your Board's evaluation may reveal that another recipient may better support the causes that your Family Foundation focuses on.

2. Is the recipient organization well run? Unfortunately, some charitable organizations fall under poor management or become the center of misappropriation of funds or other scandal. A decline in the management standards of a recipient may warrant the ceasing of grants to that organization.

3. How do the Family Foundation's grants impact the community? Is there outward evidence that your Family Foundation is making a positive impact on the community or the persons that you ultimately intend to benefit?

4. Does your Family Foundation's gifting comply with IRS regulations requiring it to operate exclusively for charitable purposes and in accordance with its charitable mission as described in Form 1023?

To monitor these aspects, the Board may assign to its members or outside contractors the duty of visiting the recipients to see the results of its giving first hand. Some foundations require an accounting from the recipient specifying how the foundation's grant was used.

In many Family Foundations, the family expands the purpose of this evaluation to not only review the outward impact of the family's giving, but to consider the impact on the family itself. Some considerations in this context are:

- Does the Family Foundation continue to meet the charitable goals of the family members?

- Have the activities of the Family Foundation affected the dynamics and relationships of the family?

- Has the Family Foundation been successful in creating and perpetuating you or your family's legacy?

- Are the charitable goals and ideals being effectively passed to the children?

In evaluating the outward and family impact of the Family Foundation, the Mission Statement should always be the starting point. The activities and effectiveness of the Family Foundation can easily stray off course unless periodic reviews are undertaken.

COMPLYING WITH LEGAL AND TAX REGULATIONS

A Family Foundation must operate in compliance with various state and federal laws. It must also operate within the framework of its corporate bylaws or, if it is organized as a trust, its Declaration of Trust. For this reason, Board members should be familiar with the Family Foundation's organizational documents and the laws affecting its operation. The Board should also select competent legal counsel and an accountant familiar with charitable foundations.

As we discussed earlier, a Family Foundation must apply to the IRS to be recognized as a tax-exempt entity. Many of the laws are designed to ensure that the Family Foundation continues to maintain such tax-exempt status. The Family Foundation is required to file an annual income tax return and make its financial statements available for public inspection.

Many of the restrictions applying to Family Foundations are found in the Internal Revenue Code. The following is a brief summary of some of the more important ones.

THE CONCEPT OF FIDUCIARY RESPONSIBILITY

Board members of a Family Foundation, including trustees, directors, and officers are considered to be fiduciaries under the law. A fiduciary is a person charged with the duty of acting for the benefit of another party. The Board member is a fiduciary because he is acting for the benefit of the donors and beneficiaries of the Family Foundation. He has been put in a position of trust and reliance that calls for a higher standard.

The law requires fiduciaries to act in good faith, avoid any type of self-dealing, manage the property with reasonable care, and not abuse or take advantage of their position and the trust that has been placed in them. If a Board member violates these standards, he may be personally liable for any resulting damages.

A Board member may also be liable along with the foundation for any excise taxes or penalties resulting from making prohibited transactions. While competent legal counsel can help eliminate the risk, these are reasons why each Board member should be familiar with his duties and with the laws applying to the Family Foundation.

QUALIFYING DISTRIBUTION REQUIREMENTS

Each year, your Family Foundation is required to distribute an amount equal to 5% of its "non-charitable use" assets. The "non-charitable use" assets are the investments and funds which make up the foundation's endowment. The assets are valued at their market value computed for the previous year.

These 5% distributions are referred to as *qualifying distributions* and include grants to independent public charities as well as reasonable expenses of administering the Family Foundations. If the Family Foundation fails to distribute 5% each year, an excise tax of at least 30% will be assessed against the shortfall.

MAKING ELIGIBLE GRANTS

Your Family Foundation can only make grants to organizations that are eligible under the Internal Revenue Code to receive them. These organizations include 501(c)(3) organizations.

If the Family Foundation makes a grant to an entity not eligible to receive it, such grant will be ruled a taxable expenditure, will not count toward the 5% requirement, and may subject the Family Foundation to an excise tax. Any Board member who knowingly approves a taxable expenditure must personally pay a 5% excise tax on the amount of the expenditure.

If the Family Foundation makes a grant to a person or organization that is not an eligible charity, the Board is required to make sure that the grant is used solely for charitable purposes. This may entail a written agreement by the recipient certifying that the funds will be used for charitable purposes only and specifying that purpose and monitoring to make sure that the agreement is complied with.

SELF-DEALING

One of the most important and stringent regulations for Boards of Family Foundations is the rule of self-dealing. These rules were enacted by Congress in 1969 to address widespread misuse of foundation funds for personal rather than charitable purposes.

Basically, these rules prohibit transactions between the Family Foundation and what the law calls *"disqualified persons."* All Board members and their immediate families are considered to be disqualified persons as well as contributors and donors to the Family Foundation and entities in which the Family Foundation has a greater than 20% interest. It also includes corporations or companies in which disqualified persons have more than 35% ownership.

The prohibited transactions include loans, leases and sales of products or services. For example, under these rules a Family Foundation cannot lease office space from a board member or other disqualified person or an entity owned more than 35% by disqualified persons. This prohibition is absolute, which means that it is not allowed even if the terms of the lease are fair and reasonable.

The IRS takes these rules against self-dealing very seriously. Penalties may be levied against both the disqualified person and the Family Foundation and may be severe. Also, any Board member who knowingly and willfully participates in a self-dealing transaction will be penalized.

The rules against self-dealing do not prohibit hiring family members or other disqualified persons. The law provides an exception for this provided the services performed in the job are necessary in carrying out the Family Foundation's charitable purpose and the salary or compensation is reasonable (not more than you would pay a non-disqualified person for the same job).

RULES REGARDING INVESTMENTS

Board members must exercise ordinary care and prudence in selecting and managing the Family Foundation's investments. Elsewhere in the course we discuss the creation of an investment strategy for the foundation. One of the most important concerns in developing and executing that strategy is the prohibition against "*jeopardy investments*."

Jeopardy investments are those investments that jeopardize the ability of the Family Foundation to carry out its charitable purposes. The IRS does not specify jeopardy investments, but leaves it open to judgment based on certain guidelines. The foundation laws provide certain benefits for organizations and donors who engage in charitable activities. In return, and to protect the charities and the ultimate beneficiaries, restrictions are placed on the activities of the foundations. The jeopardy investment rules are designed to prevent foundations from investing in a risky manner.

Whether an investment is a jeopardy investment is determined using the "prudent investor" standard. This standard requires the investor to exercise common business care and prudence, considering the facts and circumstances existing at the time the investment is made, in providing for the long-term and short-term financial needs of the foundation to carry out its charitable purpose.

If the IRS determines that the Family Foundation has engaged in jeopardy investments, it may be subject to excise taxes of 10% of the amount of the jeopardy investment. The Board is also required to change the investment so that it is no longer a jeopardy investment.

EXCESS BUSINESS HOLDINGS

Families that create Family Foundations must be careful how they fund the foundation. A Family Foundation is generally permitted to hold no more than 20% of the voting stock of any corporation. This is reduced by the percentage of such stock owned by a disqualified person. For example, if a disqualified person owns 15% of ABC Corporation, then the Family Foundation can own only 5% of the corporation.

Families that donate stock in a closely held corporation to the Family Foundation will likely violate this rule, as the family members who are disqualified persons will normally own more than 20% of the stock themselves.

The rule against excess business holdings does have two exceptions:

> 1. If one or more non-disqualified persons have effective control of the corporation, then the Family Foundation and all disqualified persons together may own up to 35% of the voting stock.

> 2. A Family Foundation is not considered to have excess business holdings in a corporation in which it owns no more than 2% of the voting stock and no more than 2% of the value of all outstanding shares of all classes of stock.

A Family Foundation may hold non-voting stock of a corporation provided that all disqualified persons together hold no more than 20% (or 35% in the case of exception one above) of the voting stock.

If a Family Foundation or disqualified persons obtain voting shares of a corporation and this causes the Family Foundation to exceed the allowable percentage, the Family Foundation has five years to reduce the holdings to a permissible amount or pay an excise tax on the value of the excess stock.

CREATING AND IMPLEMENTING AN INVESTMENT STRATEGY

The Board is responsible for the management of the Family Foundation's assets. In order to do so, it must create an investment strategy. Because many Family Foundations are set up to have perpetual existence, the Board members will have to plan on both a long-term and short-term basis.

The complexity of the regulations and laws involving foundation asset management and investment usually suggest retaining an investment advisor experienced in private foundations.

GOALS AND RISK TOLERANCE

The Board's first step in developing the Family Foundation's investment strategy is to set the goals for investing. Does the Board place a higher priority on preserving the initial contribution, increasing the endowment through long-term growth or maximizing income to increase to grants? Board members should also be surveyed to determine their level of risk tolerance. How comfortable is a Board member with volatility?

These considerations will help provide a basis for your Family Foundation's advisors and investment managers.

DIVERSITY

Another part of the basis for the Board's investment strategy is asset allocation. Board members must determine how the Family Foundation's assets will be divided between equities (stocks), bonds, cash and other investments.

Most Boards use financial advisors to help them determine the optimum mix of assets that provide the highest return with an acceptable amount of risk. Not only does the Board and advisor select a mix of investments for the asset allocation, they must effectively diversify investments within each asset class.

For example, if the Board determines that the best asset allocation would consist of 40% stocks, it must further diversify within the stocks to allocate among large cap stocks, small cap stocks, international equities and others. For investments in bonds and other debt instruments, diversification calls for selecting various companies and government issuers and staggering the maturity dates.

Investment and management of the Family Foundation's assets is an important aspect of fulfilling the Board's fiduciary responsibility. Strict penalties await those Boards that do not follow the rules and standards of investment for private foundations. The following suggestions will help avoid these problems:

- **Hire a Professional Investment Manager.** Unless the Board consists of one or more investment professionals, it is highly advisable to retain a professional investment manager. A good manager will be familiar with the laws applying to private foundation investments and will be able to manage the portfolio with the required diligence.

- **Constantly Evaluate the Investments.** The Board should regularly meet with the investment manager and evaluate the portfolio to make sure it meets the Family Foundation's investment strategy and keeps pace with the markets and economy.

- **Document Activities and Get Advice From Advisors in Writing.** This reflects prudent business practices and meets corporate legal requirements. When questions arise as to the Board's investment decisions, there should be a written record of the manner and considerations of the Board when making those decisions. Further, corporate law requires written minutes documenting major decisions of the Board.

MANAGING THE OPERATING FINANCES OF THE FAMILY FOUNDATION.

In addition to managing the investments of the Family Foundation, the Board is responsible for budgeting and managing the operating expenses. The expenses will include rent, equipment acquisition and maintenance, professional fees (attorneys and accountants), salaries and meeting expenses.

Many of these expenses are heavily regulated by the IRS and care must be taken in their implementation and monitoring.

FOUNDATION MANAGEMENT SERVICES.

Many investment firms and other companies offer foundation management and administrative services that take care of much of the daily management of running a Family Foundation.

The companies can provide the expertise technology and resources on an affordable basis. They take care of much of the administrative work inherent in the running of a Family Foundation, thereby reducing or eliminating the need for a staff and allowing the board to focus on the charitable mission.

LESSON SIX:

ALTERNATIVES TO FAMILY FOUNDATIONS.

As we saw, a Family Foundation is an effective method of leaving a legacy to your community. However, your circumstances may not lend themselves to such a project.

- Your estate may not be large enough to warrant the expense of creating and maintaining a Family Foundation.

- Your family may not be able or willing to continue in the management of a Family Foundation.

- You may wish to express your legacy in a simpler manner.

Because every person's circumstances are different, there are alternatives that will support your community and build your legacy. Some of these alternatives are:

1.   Donor Advised Funds
2.   Supporting Organizations
3.   Charitable Gift Annuities

DONOR ADVISED FUNDS

A Donor Advised Fund is a charitable fund generally set up through a Community Foundation. Many investment companies, such as Fidelity, also offer the resources to set up a Donor Advised Fund. I will refer to Community Foundations in this article, but you should keep in mind that most of these principles apply to the investment companies also. A Donor Advised Fund is an alternative to a Family Foundation for those who do not want to take on the responsibility of administration, potential liability, record keeping and lack of privacy. Since Donor Advised Funds are set up and administered through Community Foundations, a good starting place would be a definition and discussion of Community Foundation.

What is a Community Foundation?

A Community Foundation is a public charity organized under the Internal Revenue Code. They are generally set up to serve a specific geographical area. Community Foundations provide grants to a number of different charities in its service area. Instead of concentrating on one charitable cause, a Community Foundation dedicates itself to serving the wide variety of needs of its community and donors.

Community Foundations are set up as endowments and the grants given by it come solely from the income of those endowments. Many Community Foundations limit the amount of grants they can give each year to a specific percentage of the endowment principal. In this way, the endowment remains stable during times of market volatility.

In setting up a Donor Advised Fund, you would donate a sum of money or property to the Community Foundation as a permanently endowed fund. Each year the income from your fund would be available to contribute to charitable organizations or causes in the community. You and your family are allowed to direct or advise how the grants are to be distributed each year.

Comparison of Donor Advised Funds with Family Foundations.

1. Donor Control.

Both Family Foundations and Donor Advised Funds provide the donor with various levels of control in selecting grant recipients. With a Donor Advised

Fund, you and your family, as the donor, can make advisory recommendations to the Community Foundation which has the ultimate authority to select the recipients.

As we saw earlier in this course, with a Family Foundation, you have complete control in selecting grant recipients (subject, of course, to IRS requirements). Founders can create their own board, have a wide choice of investments and absolute discretion in recipients. Family Foundations allow you the full range of flexibility and control.

2. Set Up Costs.

Donor Advised Funds are much less expensive to create than Family Foundations. Family Foundations require the formation of an entity, either a nonprofit corporation or a trust, with all of the appropriate legal fees and filing costs. The Donor Advised Fund is created within the Community Foundation and, in most cases, can be set up with a simple agreement.

3. Record Keeping and Administration.

Management, record keeping and tax reporting for a Donor Advised Fund is provided by the Community Foundation usually at a low annual fee (1% of less of the fund balance). The board of a Family Foundation has the responsibility of administering the

Family Foundation, although as we have discussed, they can retain outside management services.

4. **Charitable Tax Deductions.**

With a Donor Advised Fund, cash contributions are deductible at the full rate (up to 50% of the donor adjusted gross income "AGI"). Family Foundations' tax deductions are limited to up to 30% of the AGI. Contributions to Donor Advised Funds of marketable securities and other property such as real estate receive a charitable tax deduction for the full market value. With Family Foundations, the deduction for marketable securities is based on the full market value. However, for other appreciated property, like real estate, the deduction is limited to the donor's cost bases in the property.

5. **Excise Taxes.**

Family Foundations are required to pay a 2% annual excise tax on its net investment income. Donor Advised Funds are not subject to this tax.

For persons with smaller estates or those that do not require the control over the grant making process, a Donor Advised Fund is an attractive alternative.

Donor Advised Funds provide much more privacy. Because of the need for tax filings and reporting with the Family Foundation, it is easier for people to find out the identity of donors and how much money they contribute. The amount of an individual's contribution to a Donor Advised Fund is not publicly available.

ESTABLISHING A DONOR ADVISED FUND

1. <u>WRITE A FAMILY MISSION STATEMENT.</u>

The initial step of establishing a Donor Advised Fund is the same as those for creating a Family Foundation. Before going any further, go back and read STEP ONE: DEVELOP A GIVING STRATEGY under the section for CREATING A FAMILY FOUNDATION.

Your family giving strategy is the basis for any charitable giving you do, whether it is by creating a Family Foundation, setting up a Donor Advised Fund, leaving a charitable bequest in your Will, or just making a present charitable gift.

2. <u>FIND AND EVALUATE A COMMUNITY FOUNDATION IN THE COMMUNITY YOU WISH TO SERVE.</u>

After developing a giving strategy for you and your family, the next step is to find a Community Foundation to work with. The Council on Foundations has a website that has a list of all the Community Foundations in the United States with a locator page that can segment them by state or postal code (www.cof.org). Most Community Foundations serve a specific geographical area, so it is important to match the service area with the community you wish to benefit.

In evaluating whether a particular community Foundation is right for you, the following factors may be considered:

1. Size. Does the Community Foundation have an asset base that will adequately serve the community? Is the fund growing or decreasing? You should be assured that the Community Foundation is fiscally sound and has sufficient resources to make an impact on the community for years to come.

2. Reputation. Does the Community Foundation have an impeccable reputation in the area? Most Community Foundations select their board members from prominent members of the community. The people who are selected to guide the Community Foundation say a lot about the organization itself. Research the Community Foundation practices and effectiveness. Speak with local professionals such as attorneys, accountants and financial advisors. Many have clients who have set up funds or worked with the Community Foundation. While confidentiality standards will probably prevent them from giving you specifics, they may be happy to share their overall impressions of the Foundation with you.

Talk with other charitable organizations within the community, especially those that address the needs and causes you favor. Many of these organizations look to the Community Foundation for grants and support. They will be able to tell you how it is to work with the Foundation from the perspective.

3. Similarity of Mission Statements. Read the Community Foundation's Mission Statement and service standards. Do they match your goals and ideas.

4. Personality. Finally, meet with the staff of the Community Foundation. Many have separate departments for donors and grant recipients. Make sure you speak with both. Other factors to discuss are:

- **Investment Policy.** How does the Community Foundation invest its endowment? Who is responsible for these decisions? What is their track record? Will the Foundation allow you to select your own advisor to manage your particular fund? If so, what are the guidelines and restrictions?

- **Fees and Costs.** What are the expenses and fees associated with setting up and managing your Donor Advised Fund?

- **What Assets Does the Foundation Accept?** Does the Community Foundation accept real estate? Artwork? Limited Partnership Interest? If they don't accept an appreciated asset in its existing form, personally liquidating that asset may result in adverse tax consequences.

- **Restrictions on Grants.** Is there a minimum or maximum grant amount? Are grants restricted to organizations located in a specific geographic area?

- **Duration.** Will the Donor Advised Fund continue in perpetuity after your death? Does perpetuity require a minimum contribution?

3. ENTER INTO A DONOR ADVISED FUND AGREEMENT.

Once you have chosen a Community Foundation, you should meet with the staff and plan your Donor Advised Fund. The staff should be able to answer questions and provide information on the needs of the community, strategies that can help you maximize your tax benefits, and provide a giving program that makes the most of your contributions.

Consult with your professional advisors, such as your attorney, accountant and financial advisor, to review the information and recommendations you obtained from the staff.

Your Donor Advised Fund is created by an agreement between you and the Community Foundation. This agreement sets forth the terms by which you will contribute funds and the Community Foundation will distribute grants.

Many Donor Advised Funds are created as a **testamentary** fund. This means it will be funded after the Donor's death. This is usually accomplished by a bequest from the Donor's Will or revocable trust, death benefits from a life insurance policy, or transfer on death from a bank or investment account.

The fund can also be created and funded during the donor's lifetime. In that case, you can take advantage of the charitable income tax deductions we discussed earlier. You can also enjoy seeing the impact your generosity is making on the community.

You should designate a name for your Donor Advised Fund. The fund name should include your name or your family's name to preserve your legacy. Examples are: The Fred and Wilma Flintstone Scholarship Fund or The Addam's Family Endowment Fund. The name of the fund can describe its purpose such as the scholarship fund above or The Homer Simpson Endowment Fund for the Arts.

Each agreement should also specify the purpose of the fund. This section is important because it is where the Community Foundation agrees to use your fund and make grants for the charitable cause you wish to benefit.

Remember, unlike the Family Foundation, you will not have the absolute authority to select the grant recipients. The tax law only allows you and your named successors to make grant recommendations for gifts from the fund you establish. As a result, it is critical that you state the purpose of your fund as clearly and succinctly as you can.

The agreement also contains a provision governing gifts or donations to the fund. It allows you or anyone on your behalf to make contributions to the Community Foundation in the name of your fund. It also specifies, as required by tax law, that the Community Foundation has legal control over the funds contributed to it. In order to you to get the full charitable deduction, you cannot retain control over the money or property that you contribute. This contract provision provides the basis for your deduction.

The distribution clause authorizes the Community Foundation to make distributions to the grant recipients. You will notice that there is nothing giving the donor the authority to choose the grant recipient. Based on Federal tax law, the Community Foundation must have full authority to make that choice. The donor has the ability to make recommendations for the recipients. As a practical matter, unless there is a legal or ethical reason to do otherwise, the Community Foundation will honor the recommendations of the donor. However, the donor must give up all control in the fund in order to fully partake in the tax benefits.

The burden of and authority to manage the funds rest solely with the Community Foundation. This section verifies that it will administer the Donor Advisor Fund in compliance with state and federal law.

Each agreement specifies the duration of the Donor Advised Fund. Generally, it is set up to continue for as long as there are available funds. Other circumstances may call for the fund to pay out after a set number of years.

The Community Foundation has all authority and bears all liability for the investment of the funds, including those attributed to your Donor Advised Funds.

Each Community Foundation has a written set of investment standards. You should request a copy, take the time to read it, and discuss it with the staff.

It is common practice for the Community Foundation to work with one or more professional investment managers who will invest and manage the funds of the Community Foundation in accordance with the investment standards. The board of directors of the Community Foundation has the ultimate authority and liability over the investment of the funds. Some Community Foundations will allow your financial advisor to have a role in the investment of your fund's assets. You should discuss this issue with the staff if you want a particular investment advisor involved.

Most agreements require that you agree that your Donor Advised Fund is responsible for a share of the administrative costs of the Community Foundation. Some Community Foundations have separate funds that were set up by donors for the sole purpose of paying administrative expenses of the Community Foundation. This has the effect of reducing or eliminating each individual fund's burden of these expenses. Inquire of the staff about the existence of such a fund.

4. SELECT YOUR RECOMMENDATIONS FOR GRANT RECIPIENTS.

You will recall that you, as the Donor of the Donor Advised Fund, have authority only to recommend the recipients of the grants to the Community Foundation. According to IRS regulations, the Community Foundation must make the final determinations. For this reason, it is important to acquire and understand the Community's Foundation's requirements and procedures for selecting grant recipients.

Most Community Foundations require your recommendation to be in writing. Some may have specific timetables; others receive the recommendations at any time.

The staff then reviews the recommendation to determine whether it meets their criteria. The first test requires that an organization recipient be a bona fide charitable organization recognized by the IRS.

Recipient organizations must provide an exemption letter and certain financial information or the law prevents the grant from being made.

The staff may also have additional criteria for the recipient organization to meet. You should put together a list of possible recipients that reflect your mission statement prior to creating your Donor Advised Fund and have the Community Foundation review it. In that way, they can warn you if an organization you prefer does not meet their criteria.

Some possible criteria may include the following:

1. Location. Many Community Foundations have a defined service area. They may require that the grant from your Donor Advised Fund impact the residents of their service area. Most Community Foundations prefer that the grants remain in the service area, but will allow you to contribute outside if that if your intention.

2. Reputation. Some Community Foundations will discourage gifts to organizations that have misapplied funds or otherwise engaged in illegal or unethical behavior. Again, this is an issue that can be discussed with staff before setting up your fund.

3. Size. Grant recommendations often must meet a minimum amount. The paperwork and man-hours that go into making a grant suggest that the grant be large enough to make the process efficient. Many Community Foundations have annual spending limits for their unrestricted funds, but generally allow you to make recommendations of any size up to the full value of your Donor Advised Fund.

5. <u>PROVIDE FOR CONTINUITY</u>.

The advisory rights of Donor Advised Funds are usually limited to the donor, the donor's spouse, and certain specifically-named successors. The right to recommend grants will end with the death or incapacity of the last of these persons. After that time, the Community Foundation will make all grant decisions following the purpose you stated in the Donor Advised Fund Agreement.

This is an important distinction from a Family Foundation which allows the Board to be selected each year for the life of the Foundation.

The Community Foundation manages your Donor Advised Fund under the agreement and does not want to be forced to deal with future family members who may be at odds with one another. Some Community Foundations will allow you to name a series of successor advisors, but this must be specified in advance.

SUPPORTING ORGANIZATION

Another alternative to Family Foundations and Donor Advised Funds is the Supporting Organization. A Supporting Organization is an entity you create which is affiliated with a Community Foundation. Because it is affiliated with and "supports" the Community Foundation, it is classified as a public charity and you receive the same charitable deduction for contributions as you do with a Donor Advised Fund.

Unlike a Donor Advised Fund, the Supporting Organization is a separate entity from the Community Foundation. It has its own Board, bylaws, and makes its own decisions. Most Community Foundations allow Supporting Organizations to use their investment management services.

The Board of a Supporting Organization has complete control over the selection of grant recipients and the timing and size of grants subject to IRS regulations and, in some cases, the policies of the Community Foundation.

Even though the Supporting Organization is a separate entity and has a great deal of control over its investments and grant making, it is not treated as a private foundation and is not subject to the many IRS requirements that affect the Family Foundation. The chart on the next pages compares the three funds we have discussed.

	PRIVATE FOUNDA-TION	DONOR ADVISED FUND	SUPPORTING ORGANIZA-TION
Tax Exempt Status	Must apply for private foundation status from IRS.	Shares the public charity tax-exempt status of Community Foundation	Shares the pubic charity tax-exempt status of Community Foundation as an affiliate organization
Control	Trustees have complete control of distributions (subject to IRS) and investments	Donor can make grant recommendations cannot control investments	Donor appoints board (with Community Foundation) which makes all decisions

Cost	Start-up costs, annual operating costs for management, legal, accountting, etc.	No start-up costs, pays Community Foundation management fee.	No start-up costs, pays Community Foundation management fee.
Formation	Non-profit corp. - must file organizing documents with state Trust- must draft Declaration of Trust	Establish with simple agreement	Corporation created with assistance from Community Foundation
Deductibility of Cash Gifts	Tax deduction of up to 30% AGI. Tax deduction for FMV of marketable securities, all other appreciated property limited to donor's cost basis	Tax deduction of up to 50% AGI. Tax deduction for full FMV of marketable securities and other appreciated property	Tax deduction of up to 50% AGI. Tax deduction for full FMV of marketable securities and other appreciated property

Deductibility for Appreciated Property	Up to 20% of AGI	Up to 30% of AGI	Up to 30% of AGI
Payout Requirements	Must pay out at least 5% of value each year regardless of income	No requirement. Spending policy made by donor	No requirement. Spending policy made by Board
Federal Taxes	Subject to excise tax of up to 2% of net investment gain	None	None

Involvement of Successor Generations	In perpetuity as set by Board's policies	Limited to those living when fund is created.	In perpetuity as set by Board's policies
Anonymity (if desired)	No - Must file tax and information-al returns on donations, investments, grants, expenses, etc.	Yes - Donors and grants may be kept private. Community Foundation files the reports.	Yes - Donors and grants may be kept private. Community Foundation files the reports.
Annual Tax Filings	Must file IRS Form 990-PF with required schedules	No filings required. (Community Foundation includes with its filings)	Must file IRS Form 990. Usually obtains assistance from Community Foundation
Fiduciary Responsi-bilities	Board has full fiduciary responsibility	Donor has no fiduciary responsibility. Community Foundation assumes it all.	Board has limi-ted fiduciary responsibility. Community Foundation assumes some.
Main Advantages	Complete Control Deductibility (limited) Employment of Family Independence Ability to Manifest a Lasting Legacy	Full Deductibility Flexibility Management Assistance Longevity	Full Deductibility Separate Board Management Assistance Limited Control Family Identity

LESSON SEVEN:

FUNDING YOUR CHARITABLE LEGACY

YOUR LEGACY AND YOUR ESTATE PLANNING.

Our society encourages charitable giving. Even to the extent that our government provides significant tax benefits for it. In fact, many of these tax benefits are so favorable that they create valuable opportunities for you to support a cause you believe in, establish a legacy for you and your family, reduce your income and estate taxes, and provide tax-free distributions to your heirs.

Sounds too good to be true? Fear not, it is true. One particular plan we will discuss is the ultimate win-

win scenario. It makes everyone happy – the charitable cause, you (the donor and taxpayer), and even the IRS. In fact, not only does the government accept this plan, it specifically guides you in how to do it in the IRS Regulations. This plan involves use of a Charitable Remainder Trust which I will discuss in detail in a few pages.

Whether you employ the use of one of these plans or not, your charitable legacy should work in conjunction with your estate planning. Consider your charitable cause as another one of your heirs. Only this is an heir that can provide you with tremendous tax advantages and the substance upon which to build your legacy. Properly planning for this special heir can open up opportunities to provide for your family and yourself that would not have existed without it. It may sound improbable, but including charitable giving in your estate plan can actually increase the amounts you will leave to your family **and** increase your net income during your lifetime. And in many instances, your charitable giving will only use money that would have gone to the government in taxes otherwise.

So, without further ado, let's look at some different options you have to fund your charitable legacy.

FUNDING OPTION ONE:

THE DIRECT GIFT.

The simplest and most direct form of charitable giving is a direct gift. You make a present gift to the charitable organization or cause of your choice. It's pure and simple: you see a need and you help fill it.

The direct gift has its advantages. You can be responsive to a community need or you can make the gifts systematically. Most times, you have the opportunity to see the impact of your philanthropy.

You may gift any type of property you wish: cash, stocks, or real estate, and your receive a charitable deduction against your income.

Present gifts can be combined with planned giving programs to supplement your charitable strategy. For example, you can make a gift to a Family Foundation or Donor Advised Fund you have set up.

There are also certain tactics you can employ to increase tax benefits. You can time your gifts so as to apply the deduction against specific income.

Another tactic involves highly appreciated property such as real estate or stock. I realize that, at the time I write this, the condition of the real estate and stock markets make it hard to fathom a highly appreciated asset, but they do exist! In fact, today's conditions provide the opportunity for you to realize substantial increases in the future.

For example, you purchased shares of a particular stock at a total price of $100,000, and now, five years later, it is worth $300,000. You are also looking to make a $300,000 gift to your favorite charitable organization, as you feel that good fortune has smiled on you and you wish to share it with others less fortunate. Some people would liquidate the stock and write a check for $300,000 to the organization. They are pleased with these events. They were able to help make a difference in others' lives, they contributed money that they didn't require to live on, and they received a nice charitable deduction. However, by selling the stock, they also realized a $200,000 capital gain which will be taxable at that year's capital gains tax rate. Now, to make the $300,000 gift, they have to expend more than $300,000.

A more efficient scenario would have been to give the shares of stock directly to the charitable organization. The charity would receive the same benefit; however, because you gifted the stock without first liquidating it, you did not recognize any capital gain. You still received the charitable deduction for the full amount.

The charitable organization would then liquidate the stock and, because of its charitable status, would not incur capital gains tax. Your entire $300,000 would benefit the need you chose.

(Caveat: If the gift is real estate or an appreciated asset other than marketable securities and the gift is made to your Family Foundation, your charitable deduction would be limited to your costs basis – $100,000 in the above example – of the gifted asset.)

FUNDING OPTION TWO:

BEQUESTS AND POST-DEATH GIFTS.

Another method of giving to a charity is through a bequest in you will or distribution from an inter vivos trust. Your bequest or distribution can be made in a number of ways. You can leave a cash bequest of a specific amount to the charitable organization. Or you can leave a particular property such as a parcel of real property, you home or personal property. Finally, you can make a bequest of the residuary of your estate where the organization receives the remainder of the estate (or a stated percentage of the remainder) after specific bequests and expenses of administration have been paid.

Other post-death gifts include naming the charitable organization as a beneficiary on your life insurance policy, annuity or retirement plan (such as an IRA or 401(k)).

A charitable gift made at death is excluded from your estate for estate tax purposes, but you do not receive any income tax benefits. You do, however, retain the money and property in case you would need it during your lifetime.

The post-death gifts can also be made to your Family Foundation Donor, Advised Fund or Supporting Organization as well as outright to the charity.

FUNDING OPTION THREE:

SPLIT INTEREST GIFTS.

A funding vehicle that gives you the best of both worlds of a lifetime transfer and a post-death gift is the split interest gift. It is called "split interest" because their terms provide that the income and principal are to be distributed between two different types of beneficiaries. They can provide income to the donor and his family and the principal will be distributed to a charitable organization.

CHARITABLE GIFT ANNUITIES.

Perhaps the best way to explain the split interest gift is to describe an actual example. A simple, yet effective form of split interest gift is the Charitable Gift Annuity.

With a Charitable Gift Annuity, you transfer property (cash, investments, real estate or personal property) to a charitable organization. In return, the charitable organization promises to pay you an annuity which is calculated as a percentage of the amount you transferred. For example, if you paid $100,000 to a charity, and the terms of the Charitable Gift Annuity call for payments of 8%, you would receive $8,000 per year. Generally, such payments would continue for the rest of your life (or your spouse's life, if longer). At that time, the remaining principal stays with the charitable organization.

There are many tax benefits with a Charitable Gift Annuity.

1. **Charitable Deduction Against Income Tax.** If the amount you contribute to the Charitable Gift Annuity is greater than the cost of a regular (non-charitable) commercial annuity, the excess amount is treated as a charitable contribution and you receive a deduction. This deduction can even be applied against the payments you receive from the Charitable Gift Annuity.

2. Other Income Tax Advantages. The portion of your gift that is not treated as a charitable contribution is treated as being invested in the annuity. Within each payment you receive, a portion is treated as a tax-free return of capital. So only a portion of your payment received is taxable income. And it may be reduced by the charitable deduction you receive.

3. Even More Income Tax Advantages. If you contribute appreciated property to purchase the Charitable Gift Annuity, you would realize a capital gain. This capital gain would be pro-rated within your payments from the Charitable Gift Annuity. Therefore, a portion of the payment you receive will be taxed as capital gains and taxed at the lower capital gains rate.

Now, let's put all of these tax advantages together in the following example.

You purchase a Charitable Gift Annuity from a Community Foundation by transferring $500,000 of stock that you originally purchased for $100,000. The terms of the Charitable Gift Annuity provide for annual payments of 6% or $30,000 to you. Based on your age, you will receive an income tax deduction for the contribution. In this case, we will assume a deduction of $150,000 for the year your purchased the Charitable Gift Annuity. This translates to an income tax savings of $45,000 if you are in the 30 percent tax bracket. As for the breakdown of your payments: each year you will receive a $30,000 payment. Of this, $11,501 will be taxed as capital gains, $168.61 will be a tax-free return of principal, leaving $18,330 to be taxed as ordinary income, against which you may apply your charitable deduction.

In addition to the tax benefits, there are advantages which Charitable Gift Annuities.

- Your payout from the Charitable Gift Annuity can begin immediately or be deferred. In that way, you can purchase an annuity now and apply the deduction while your income is high. You can defer the payments until later to supplement your retirement income.

- The Charitable Gift Annuity provides a guaranteed, fixed payment for your lifetime, or for the lifetimes of you and your spouse.

- In the case of appreciated assets, your payout would be based on the market value of the assets. Without the Charitable Gift Annuity, you would have to sell the asset, pay the capital gains tax and invest the remaining amount to get your return.

- When the Charitable Gift Annuity matures, the remaining principal will fund a permanent legacy for you and your family which will benefit others for years to come.

THE CHARITABLE REMAINDER TRUST

To many, the scenario I am about to describe is too good to be true. Let's start by listing the benefits of planning with a Charitable Remainder Trust (or CRT) by showing how it can solve problems you may encounter.

Problem: You have a piece of real estate that is producing no income for you. You would like to sell it and reinvest the proceeds to create a regular income, but the real estate has greatly appreciated since you purchased it and you don't want to be hit with massive capital gains taxes.

Problem: You want to create a legacy by funding a scholarship fund for disadvantaged students in your community, but the piece of real estate is the only asset you can use to fund the scholarship fund. You also wanted to use a part of the real estate to fund your children's inheritance.

How can you sell the real estate, use the proceeds to invest and provide yourself a stable income, use the proceeds to set up a scholarship fund after your death **and** provide for your children's inheritance? The answer is the Charitable Remainder Trust. To show you how this works, let's look at a fictional example:

In 1995, you and your spouse purchased a piece of vacant commercial real estate for $100,000. Lately, you have received offers of $1,100,000 for the property from a developer who wants to build a shopping center on it. You currently receive no income from the property. To the contrary, you have annual expenses for property taxes and liability insurance.

If you sell the property to the developer, you will have a capital gain of $1,000,000 (sales price of $1,100,000 less you $100,000 tax basis in the property). At a 15% capital gains rate, you would pay $150,000 in capital gains tax, leaving only $950,000 to reinvest. If you invest it at a 7% annual rate, you will receive $66,500 each year in income which will be taxed at your ordinary income tax rate. When you and your spouse have both passed away, whatever is left of the $950,000 after estate taxes can be divided between your children and the scholarship fund.

Now, let's insert the Charitable Remainder Trust into the equation. Instead of selling the real estate to the developer, you can create a CRT and donate the real estate to it. The CRT would then sell the real estate to the developer. Since it is a charitable entity, the CRT does not pay the capital gains tax. As a result, the entire $1,100,000 is available to invest.

With a Charitable Remainder Trust, you can specify what percentage return you want to receive (provided the return falls within limits determined by a number of factors, including your age). A higher return to you would reduce the amount ultimately donated to the scholarship fund and conversely a lower return would increase the donation.

Let's say you choose the 7% rate we used above. You will receive $77,000 in income each year, an increase of $10,500 from the example without the CRT. This amount would be paid to you and your spouse for a long as one of you survives.

It gets even better. In addition to the increased annual income, you will receive a charitable deduction toward your income for a portion of the contribution you made to the CRT. Since part of the contribution you made will come back to you and your spouse as an annual income, you will not receive a deduction for the entire $1,100,000. Your tax advisor would determine the present value of the total income you and your spouse would receive from the CRT based on your life expectancy and subtract that amount from your total contribution to arrive at your charitable deduction. This deduction can be applied against your CRT income, further increasing your after tax income.

Upon the death of the survivor of you and your spouse, all of the assets then in the CRT will be paid to your designated charity.

But that's not all. Using the tax savings created by the charitable deduction plus a portion of the increase in annual income, you can establish a wealth replacement trust for the purpose of acquiring a second-to-die life insurance policy that will provide a tax-free inheritance for your children. The increased income you receive as a result of the CRT can be used to fund the insurance premiums.

This is a win-win-win situation. You and your spouse win with these benefits:

1. No Capital Gains Tax on the Sale of the Real Estate
2. Charitable Income Tax Deduction
3. Increased Annual Income
4. Eliminate or Reduce Estate Tax
5. Manifest a Legacy in the Community

Your children or other heirs win with the following benefits:

1. No Reduction in their Inheritance
2. No Probate
3. They Receive their Inheritance in Tax-Free Cash

The community wins because you have made a significant contribution that will make a difference in other people's lives.

The only non-winner is the IRS. And believe it or not, it endorses the Charitable Remainder Trust wholeheartedly. In fact, the Treasury Regulations instruct you in detail how to set up a CRT. Imagine that!

A BRIEF PRIMER ON CHARITABLE REMAINDER TRUSTS.

A Charitable Remainder Trust is an irrevocable split-interest trust. Irrevocable means that once it is set up, it cannot be terminated at the discretion of the creator (Grantor). Also, property contributed to the trust is permanently removed from the Grantor's estate. If he needs to take back the property later, he will not be able to do so, although he can provide for income payments to himself for life.

Split-interest means that the property in the trust is shared between non-charitable beneficiaries and charitable beneficiaries. Usually, the CRT pays income to one or more non-charitable beneficiaries (typically, the Grantor and spouse) for their lifetimes or for a specified number of years - not to exceed 20. At the death of the last income beneficiary or after the specified number of years expires, all property remaining in the trust must be distributed to one or more charities.

A CRT is exempt from income, capital gain and estate taxes. The donor or grantor receives a charitable income tax deduction for the portion of the contribution that will eventually be distributed to the charity. This amount is determined by a complex IRS formula.

Any assets you contribute to the CRT can be sold by the CRT without any capital gains tax.

You can receive more income from the asset than you did before donating it to the CRT.

You can set up a wealth replacement trust to purchase a life insurance policy to replace the inheritance that was lost as a result of the CRT.

Even though the Charity will not receive its gift until later, because your contribution is irrevocable, you can manifest your legacy during your lifetime and receive recognition for your gift.

HOW LARGE MUST YOUR ESTATE BE FOR A CRT?

An attractive aspect of Charitable Remainder Trusts is that you don't have to have a large estate to benefit from it. While those who have estates large enough to worry about estate taxes can use the CRT to reduce or eliminate those taxes, those with smaller estates can take advantage of numerous opportunities.

Anyone can increase the income from their investments by transferring highly-appreciated, under performing assets to a CRT to lock in an attractive return without losing a part of the investment to capital gains taxes.

Just about any type of property can be contributed to a Charitable Remainder Trust. As we discussed, highly-appreciated assets provide the most benefit, but cash, stock, real estate and personal property (such as valuable collections) are proper.

CRTS AND RETIREMENT PLANS.

Many people have large retirement funds such as 401(k) plans or Individual Retirement Accounts. These funds have been able to grow rapidly because the government allows you to defer payment of income tax on the earnings until later (usually ago 70½).

The problems arise when the time comes to start removing the funds from the retirement plan. These problems become even worse after the death of the owner and the beneficiaries start to take funds out. For owners with large estates, the retirement plan is subject to estate tax. If all or a portion of the plan needs to be liquidated to pay estate taxes, the beneficiary is hit with the income tax that has been deferred during the owner's lifetime. Sometimes, with estate and income taxes, these assets can be taxed at rates of 60% to 70% for the highest tax bracket.

For this reason, an IRA, 401(k), or other qualified retirement plan is a great asset on which to name the CRT as beneficiary. You are not legally able to transfer the retirement plan into the CRT during your lifetime; however, you can name the CRT as the beneficiary. In that case, the income taxes due on the distributions received by the CRT are cancelled by the charitable deduction.

You can set up the CRT to leave your surviving spouse or children an income for life, with income tax payable only on the amounts actually distributed to them. You then can name a charitable organization or organizations of your choice to receive the property remaining in the CRT at your spouse's (or children's) death, which otherwise would, in large part, go to the IRS in taxes.

CRATS AND CRUTS

There are two different types of Charitable Remainder Trusts: the Charitable Remainder Annuity Trust, or CRAT, and the Charitable Remainder Unitrust, or CRUT. In most aspects, the two trusts are the same. This difference between the CRAT and the CRUT is the way the annual income distributions to the non-charitable beneficiaries are calculated.

A Charitable Remainder Annuity Trust pays a fixed annual income based on the value of the property initially transferred into the CRAT. Therefore, if you create a CRAT, contribute $100,000 to start it, and set up an 8% annual distribution, you would receive $8,000 each year. Regardless of whether the value of the property in the trust goes up or goes down, you will still receive $8,000 each year because that is 8% of the original contribution. Even if the property in the CRAT does not earn 8%, you will receive the same $8,000. In that case, a part of the principal would be invaded to make the distribution. On the other hand, if the CRAT property earned more than 8%, you would still only receive the $8,000 annual payment.

A Charitable Remainder Unitrust pays a fixed percentage based on the value of the property in trust. However, with a CRUT, the property is valued each and every year to determine the amount distributed.

For example, if you set up the CRUT with an initial contribution of $100,000 and select an 8% distribution rate, you will receive $8,000 in distributions during the first year. At the end of the first year (and each year after), the property is revalued. If the investments in the CRUT increased in value to $110,000, you would receive $8,800 during the next year. If, however, the value of the assets decreased to $90,000, you would only receive $7,200 during the next year. This process would be repeated each year.

Because the property value is redetermined each year, you can add property to a CRUT and such added property will be taken into account in determining the distribution.

You cannot add property to a CRAT after the initial contribution.

SETTING UP YOUR CHARITABLE REMAINDER TRUST

Your Charitable Remainder Trust should be set up with the help of an attorney experienced in these matters.

You should take great care in selecting the terms of the CRT since it will be irrevocable and your ability to amend the CRT will be severely limited. The persons you choose to be your income beneficiaries cannot be changed once you have signed the trust. Likewise, the annual percentage of the payments cannot be changed.

Your selection of trustee is also important. It is not a good idea for you to name yourself as trustee. If you designate yourself as trustee and as the income beneficiary, the trust property in the CRT will be included in your estate for estate tax purposes.

The trustee is responsible for investing the assets in the CRT, making the income distributions and filing the Split Interest Tax Returns with the IRS each year. The trustee must also make the distribution to the charitable organizations at the termination of the trust. Choose someone competent and trustworthy. If you are naming your Donor Advised Fund as a beneficiary, the

Community Foundation may be able to provide or arrange for trustee services.

WEALTH REPLACEMENT

Earlier I described a scenario where you can use a CRT to:

1. sell a highly appreciated asset without capital gains
2. receive a guaranteed income for life
3. receive a charitable income tax deduction
4. eliminate or reduce your estate tax
5. manifest your legacy by leaving a gift to charity at your death
6. leave an inheritance to your heirs tax free and in cash

I talked about how naming a Family Foundation or Donor Advised Fun as the charitable beneficiary can allow you to create a legacy that will benefit your community for generations to come.

Now I am going to show you how to replace the assets you have set up to leave to charity instead of your children. To do this, you would create a Wealth Replacement Trust to replace some or all of the assets you redirected to charity.

WHAT IS A WEALTH REPLACEMENT TRUST?

A Wealth Replacement Trust is an irrevocable life insurance trust that you create to own a life insurance policy insuring your life. If you are married, it can own a second-to-die policy insuring the lives of both you and your spouse.

Since the CRT usually produces increased income to you and provides savings in income taxes from the charitable deduction you receive from the contribution to the CRT, you can use this as a source to pay all or part of the premiums.

Upon your death (or the death of the last of you and your spouse), the proceeds of the life insurance policy will be paid to the Wealth Replacement Trust. Because the Wealth Replacement Trust is set up as an irrevocable trust, it is not included in your estate for estate tax purposes. It can distribute the entire proceeds to your children - tax free.

A Wealth Replacement Trust is an advanced planning technique with estate tax, gift tax and state law issues. You should seek the services of an experienced attorney to help you structure and implement this plan.

START MANIFESTING YOUR LEGACY

This course provides you with the tools to manifest a legacy for your family and your community.

The success you achieved in your life was the result of hard work, opportunity, good fortune and perhaps advice or support from others. Now you have the opportunity to contribute to the success of others. Whether by a statement of advice or encouragement or a financial investment in someone's endeavors, you can be the catalyst that propels them to success.

Make the world a better place because you have lived there.

ABOUT THE AUTHOR

Dean Hanewinckel has helped his clients with their estate planning needs for over 25 years. He practices law in Englewood, Florida.

You can find more information on creating and planning a legacy at www.manifestyourlegacy.com.

Dean is also the author of *The Official Snowbird's Guide To Becoming A Florida Resident,* the most complete resource for people moving to Florida. For more information, visit www.newfloridaresident.com .

www.ingramcontent.com/pod-product-compliance
Lightning Source LLC
Chambersburg PA
CBHW072148270326
41931CB00010B/1929